AMAZING LOVE
The Parable of the Prodigal Son

JOHN R. DE WITT

D0190493

BANNER OF TRUTH TRUST

IHE BANNER OF TRUTH TRUST
3 Murrayfield Road, Edinburgh EH12 6EL
P.O. Box 621, Carlisle, Pennsylvania 17013, USA

*

© John R. de Witt 1981
First published 1981
Reprinted 1999
ISBN 0 85151 328 X

*

Printed in Finland by WSOY

*

This edition coincides with the commemoration
by the Consistory of Seventh Reformed Church,
Grand Rapids, Michigan, USA, of the Fortieth
Anniversary of Dr John Richard de Witt's
ordination in the ministry of God's Word.

To
Greg, Jonathan
and Liza
in the hope that they will
always love
the Father's house

Contents

11 Jesus said, A certain man had two sons:

12 And the younger of them said to his father, Father, give me the portion of goods that falleth to me. And he divided unto them his living.

13 And not many days after the younger son gathered all together, and took his journey into a far country, and there wasted his substance with riotous living.

14 And when he had spent all, there arose a mighty famine in that land; and he began to be in want.

15 And he went and joined himself to a citizen of that country; and he sent him into his fields to feed swine.

16 And he would fain have filled his belly with the husks that the swine did eat: and no man gave unto him.

17 And when he came to himself, he said, How many hired servants of my father's have bread enough and to spare, and I perish with hunger!

18 I will arise and go to my father, and will say unto him, Father, I have sinned against heaven, and before thee,

19 And am no more worthy to be called thy son: make me as one of thy hired servants.

20 And he arose, and came to his father. But when he was yet a great way off, his father saw him, and had compassion, and ran, and fell on his neck, and kissed him.

21 And the son said unto him, Father, I have sinned against heaven, and in thy sight, and am no more worthy to be called thy son.

22 But the father said to his servants, Bring forth the best robe, and put it on him; and put a ring on his hand, and shoes on his feet:

23 And bring hither the fatted calf, and kill it; and let us eat, and be merry:

24 For this my son was dead, and is alive again; he was lost, and is found. And they began to be merry.

25 Now his elder son was in the field: and as he came and drew nigh to the house, he heard musick and dancing.

26 And he called one of the servants, and asked what these things meant.

27 And he said unto him, Thy brother is come; and thy father hath killed the fatted calf, because he hath received him safe and sound.

28 And he was angry, and would not go in: therefore came his father out, and intreated him.

29 And he answering said to his father, Lo, these many years do I serve thee, neither transgressed I at any time thy commandment: and yet thou never gavest me a kid, that I might make merry with my friends:

30 But as soon as this thy son was come, which hath devoured thy living with harlots, thou hast killed for him the fatted calf.

31 And he said unto him, Son, thou art ever with me, and all that I have is thine.

32 It was meet that we should make merry, and be glad: for this thy brother was dead, and is alive again; and was lost, and is found.

1. 'A Certain Man Had Two Sons'

*T*he Lord Jesus Christ was a master teacher. All who meet him in the gospel records of the New Testament have to bear witness to his consummate skill in the communication of truth. In all the history of the world there has never been a more engaging or effective teacher of men. And not the least part of his power as a teacher lay in his pointed use of parables, those superb and wonderful and apparently so simple stories which all these centuries long have continued to exercise their fascination, and which instruct and teach indeed, but which in their depth and full dimensions persist in transcending the intellectual capacity of even the most gifted and perceptive biblical scholar.

Many of us have no doubt long since learned the old children's definition of a parable: that it is an earthly story with a heavenly meaning. But good though it is, this definition does not explain the uniqueness of what Jesus was doing in his use of parables. Other teachers—the rabbis of his day, for example—also told earthly stories with a heavenly meaning. But Christ was doing something far more than that, something far more specific and significant. Thus, while it is quite true that Christ's parables are earthly stories with a heavenly meaning, yet that fails to tell us enough about them. We need to know that the stories Jesus told not only speak to us about the 'other world'—the world of spiritual reality, the world of God—but that they are also intended to reveal to us something of what God has done, and is doing, and will yet do in the present world, through and in his kingdom, by the person and work of his Son, the Lord Jesus Christ.

Of all the parables in the gospel narratives none is more affecting than that of the prodigal son, the 'forlorn son,' as Samuel Rutherford used to call him. And certainly there is no parable which is more familiar. Nearly everyone has heard at some time or other the story of the wayward boy and his father's love for him. The danger in speaking of a passage from the Bible so well-known and much-loved is that our minds will be closed to receiving new truth from it. We may too easily suppose that all the facets of the story have long since been disclosed to us, and that nothing more is to be learned from it. But to fall into that attitude is to forget the divine person who first conceived this parable, and the incapacity of any man's mind to plumb the depths of what Christ knows of God and of the heart of man.

If we stand humbly before him, eager to hear his voice afresh, there will be something new for us, a new grasp of truth, a new apprehension of spiritual reality, a new understanding of the plan of salvation, no matter how often we have heard the old word before. Christ is alive, and his word partakes of his life. 'For the word of God is quick, and powerful, and sharper than any two-edged sword, piercing even to the dividing asunder of soul and spirit, and of the joints and marrow, and is a discerner of the thoughts and intents of the heart' (Heb. 4:12). As you read, listen: not simply to me as though I had anything to say to you of myself, but to the voice and word of Christ. And remember that it is the Scriptures, and the voice of the Lord speaking through them, that are able to make us 'wise unto salvation through faith which is in Christ Jesus' (2 Tim. 3:15).

The parable begins with the words: 'And he [Jesus] said, A certain man had two sons.' We must notice first of all that *two* sons are spoken of, and not merely one. It is surely a matter of considerable significance that there is an elder brother as well as the prodigal. This expression casts us back to the opening verses of the chapter (Luke 15:1,2) where two classes of people are clearly identified, the one consisting of the publicans and sinners, the other of the Pharisees and scribes. 'Then drew near unto him all the *publicans* and *sinners* for to hear him. And the *Pharisees* and *scribes* murmured, saying, This man receiveth *sinners,* and eateth with them.'

It should be pointed out at once in this connection that both sons, and both categories, are said to be the sons of a common father. They belong together, in one family, one people. In the same way the other two parables indicate that the hundred sheep, of which one becomes lost, constitute a single flock; and the ten pieces of silver compose a single treasure. In one sense the accent is on the relatedness of the two categories: they are the sheep of the house of Israel, the children of Abraham, the heirs together of the blessings and benefits of the covenant; and as the people of God they are in a special relationship to him. But it is precisely within the framework of this relatedness, this belonging together, that judgment takes place, and that Christ speaks the distinguishing, discriminating word which is part of the great thrust of the parable—the receiving again at last of the prodigal as one alive from the dead, and the condemnation of the imperceptive, legalistic, self-righteous elder brother.

Scribes and Pharisees, publicans and sinners, are all of one national background, one high position of spiritual privilege, one outward covenant relationship to God, and it is as such in the first instance that the Lord Jesus Christ addresses them. Yet into that unity Christ drives the terrible sword of his judgment. 'The scribes and the Pharisees,' he said, 'sit in Moses' seat: all therefore whatsoever they bid you observe, that observe and do; but do not ye after their works: for they say, and do not. For they bind heavy burdens and grievous to be borne, and lay them on men's shoulders; but they themselves will not move them with one of their fingers. But all their work they do for to be seen of men. . . . But woe unto you, scribes and Pharisees, hypocrites! for ye shut up the kingdom of heaven against men; for ye neither go in yourselves, neither suffer ye them that are entering to go in. . . . Ye serpents, ye generation of vipers, how can ye escape the damnation of hell?' (Matt. 23:2-5,13,33). It is that judgment which underlies the opening words of the parable: 'A certain man had *two* sons.'

We see thus that a sharp line of demarcation is drawn in this story between these two members of a single family. The one, the prodigal, the unlikely and seemingly worthless and plainly undeserving brother, is so portrayed as to leave us in no doubt as to his position. Can anything good be said about him? He is not only the prodigal, but also the lost son. And yet it was just for such as he that our Saviour came and died, as the four gospels remind us again and again. We read, for example, that when Christ saw the multitudes, 'he was moved with compassion on them, because they fainted, and were scattered abroad, as sheep having no shepherd' (Matt. 9:36). On another occasion he said: 'I am not sent but unto the lost sheep of the house of Israel' (Matt. 15:24). 'They that be whole need not a physician, but they that are sick. But go ye and learn what that meaneth, I will have mercy, and not sacrifice: for I am not come to call the righteous, but sinners to repentance' (Matt. 9:13). And with reference now to the specific instance of Zacchaeus—a representative of the class of the publicans, the tax collectors in the employ of the hated imperial Roman government and regarded as traitors to their own people and thus as social outcasts—we find the words addessed to him: 'This day is outcasts—we find the words addressed to him: 'This day is salvation come to this house, forsomuch as he also is a to save that which was lost' (Luke 19:9-10). Christ came for the shepherdless, leaderless, kingless, saviourless, lost children of Israel, and for all among us, too, who belong with them and are in the same condition.

There is not only a contrast here, however, between the scribes and Pharisees on the one hand and the publicans and sinners on the other, in terms of the purpose of Christ's coming; one also sees a contrast between those wicked shepherds who did not feed but scattered the flock, and the Messiah of God, the Lord Jesus Christ, who came not to scatter, but to gather to himself. 'Woe be unto the pastors that destroy and scatter the sheep of my pasture! saith the Lord. Therefore thus saith the Lord God of Israel against the pastors that feed my people: Ye have scattered my flock, and driven them away, and have not visited them: behold, I will visit upon you the evil of your doings, saith the Lord. And I will gather the remnant of my flock out of all countries whither I have driven them, and will bring them again to their folds; and they shall be fruitful and increase. And I will set up shepherds over them which shall feed them: and they shall fear no more, nor be dismayed, neither shall they be lacking, saith the Lord. Behold, the days come, saith the Lord, that I will raise unto David a righteous Branch, and a King shall reign and prosper, and shall execute judgment and justice in the earth. In his days Judah shall be saved, and Israel shall dwell safely: and this is his name whereby he shall be called, THE LORD OUR RIGHTEOUSNESS' (Jer. 23:1-6; cf. Ezek. 34). 'He that is not with me', Jesus said, 'is against me; and he that gathereth not with me scattereth' (Luke 11:23).

The Pharisees, the so-called spiritual leaders of the people, did not feed the flock of God, but rather burdened them with the weight of a legalism under which in the keeping of many commandments they hoped to be saved. And when this proved to be a burden which they could not sustain, the Pharisees proceeded to declare, 'This people who knoweth not the law are cursed' (John 7:49). It is to this that our Lord refers when he says in the beautiful passage of Matthew 11:28ff., 'Come unto me, all ye that labour and are heavy laden, and I will give you rest. Take my yoke upon you, and learn of me; for I am meek and lowly in heart; and ye shall find rest unto your souls. For my yoke is easy, and my burden is light.' He intends here in the first instance not sin and care and the weight of guilt in general, but the burdensome load of a law that could not save, and of restrictions which could only bring misery and death. In speaking as he does of publicans and sinners on the one hand, therefore, and of scribes and Pharisees on the other, the Lord Jesus Christ is not extolling disobedience and sin, nor is he casting aspersions on the attempt to lead a righteous and godly life. Not at all! Rather, he is stressing and underscoring in unmistakable terms the gloriously free and gratuitous character of salvation. 'Not by works of righteousness which we have done, but according to his mercy he saved us' (Tit. 3:5). 'By grace are ye saved through faith; and that not of yourselves: it is the gift of God' (Eph. 2:8). 'For even the Son of man came not to be ministered unto, but to minister, and to give his life a ransom for many' (Mark 10:45).

But, further, there is something still more important in the opening words, 'A certain man had two sons.' Our attention is at once directed to *a certain man*. He is given no name. There is at the outset no specific indication as to who he may be. But it becomes clear as the parable progresses that under the figure of a man our Lord is speaking of One who is no man at all. The great central presupposition of the story is that there is someone behind these words, someone behind the ministry of Christ, someone active and moving and directing the course of events, someone who in important ways is like the father of the prodigal young man. And that someone is God. You see, the parable is about God, and even more specifically about God in his love and concern for men. The same thing is to be observed equally clearly in the other two parables which make up the fifteenth chapter of the Gospel of Luke—the parables of the lost sheep and the lost coin—in both of which the emphasis is upon the unweariedness and activeness and the triumphant joyfulness of the seeking and finding love of God.

The parable thus reveals to us something immensely

important about God, and his kingdom, and his method of working. We see here the sinner, wretched, lonely, estranged from the father and the father's house. And we see also the father standing by the wayside, receiving the son in mercy and forgiving him all. That, surely, is what the gospel is about: the gracious disposition of God toward men, the forgiveness of sins, the restoration of a broken relationship between creature and Creator, the casting down of the wall between them, the reconciliation of offender and Offended, with God taking the initiative and stretching out his arms in tenderness and pity, generously and benevolently inviting sinners to himself.

But we must be careful at this point, for there is one immensely important factor which is not so much as mentioned in the whole compass of the parable—Christ is not in it! And, misjudging the significance of this, some men have been led astray by an idea that the gospel—the good news of salvation, of joy, of reconciliation, of peace—can be understood without him! They have thought that the message of the Scriptures and of the Christian faith is simply one of a gracious disposition on the part of God toward his erring creatures. The accent has fallen, in this school of thought—this very mistaken, in some measure appealing, and so tragically influential school of thought —upon what has become known as the fatherhood of God and the infinite value of the soul. But the effect of it has been to underrate the seriousness of sin and of the wrath of God upon it. God is *not only* benevolent. Goodness is not his only attribute. God is also just; and the truth concerning his justice is a very solemn one, and can never be blotted out or denied. God will have his justice—his own character—to be satisfied. He will not clear the guilty. Sin is a dreadful assault upon the majesty and holiness of God, and as such it must be dealt with. Were it otherwise God would be less than God, and his goodness only an ability to overlook sin, to allow to exist unpunished that which in its very essence is a contradiction of his own nature and a violation of his holiness, righteousness, and truth. No indeed! God is not merely benevolent in the sense that, justice *unsatisfied,* he can receive sinners and admit them into fellowship with himself, their sins unpaid for, their guilt upon them still. It is the very glory and the wonder of the gospel that by Christ sin has been covered, guilt has been removed, and sinners can be declared righteous, while God remains true to himself. Thus it is that the church must always declare that a 'gospel' without Christ is no true gospel at all. Without him, without his cross, without the empty tomb he left behind him when he rose from the dead, one cannot speak of salvation or reconciliation.

We must therefore grasp very clearly what Jesus is doing in this parable, how he is able to express himself in this way. Let me quote in this connection a striking passage by one of the great evangelical New Testament scholars of our day:

> Jesus is able to proclaim the remission of sins in such a matchless way because he is not only the prophet, but also the king of the kingdom. He not only proclaims salvation, but is its bearer, and acquirer, and sharer of it with his followers.
>
> That is why there is an intrinsic connection between Jesus' preaching of the remission of sins as an act of pure divine grace and all that in his self-revelation Jesus tells about his messianic authority and mission. That which Jesus preaches about remission of sins and redemption he proclaims by virtue of his divine mis-

sion as the Son of Man to whom all power and authority has been given. And at the same time he does so as one who has to carry out all that with which he has been commissioned and that which has been written concerning him as 'the Servant of the Lord.' Salvation, including the remission of sins, is vested in his person, in the carrying out of his mission, in his obedience to the divine will.[1]

That puts the matter well and very succinctly indeed. So, while the parable of the prodigal son does not refer specifically to Christ, that is not to say there is nothing of Christ in it. Nor is it to affirm that the whole gospel can be defined upon the basis of what is said here. Rather, we should remember that what Christ is giving us in Luke 15 is an aspect of the gospel: an aspect that has to do in the first instance with the seeking, saving, finding, loving, reconciling mercy of God; and all that, furthermore, to be found in the person and work of the one telling the story. You see, while Christ is in one sense absent from the parable—there is nothing in the content of it suggestive of his passion, death, and resurrection—yet it is he who is telling the story, he from whose lips we learn of the compassion and goodness and love of the Father! The whole message of redemption upon which the story proceeds is a message vested in the highest and fullest sense in his own person and divine authority. He is the Messiah, the Christ, the Son of God, come to the lost sheep of the house of Israel and of all the world, the One come to seek and to save that which was lost. He is the reason for the story, the explanation of its possibility, the only ground and hope of salvation and life and joy.

[1]Herman N. Ridderbos, *The Coming of the Kingdom* (Philadelphia: Presbyterian and Reformed Publishing Co., 1962), p. 231.

Jesus is the revealer of God to us because he is *himself* God and the Saviour of his people.

How humble and how grateful ought we not to be before this message of patience, of compassion, of judgment not only postponed but forever cancelled for those who believe! The parable of the prodigal son is after all in the highest and holiest and deepest and grandest sense a parable of Christ, because, as the Apostle Paul tells us, 'there is therefore now no condemnation to them which are *in Christ Jesus*' (Rom. 8:1). This is the key which enables us to grasp the place and significance of the story within the framework of the proclamation of redemption. Christ is the One who gives effect to the Father's mercy and upon the basis of whose person and completed work we sinners may be saved. 'Blessed be the God and Father of our Lord Jesus Christ, who hath blessed us with all spiritual blessings in heavenly places in Christ: according as he hath chosen us in him before the foundation of the world, that we should be holy and without blame before him in love; having predestinated us unto the adoption of children by Jesus Christ to himself, according to the good pleasure of his will, to the praise of the glory of his grace, wherein he hath made us accepted in the beloved. In whom we have redemption through his blood, the forgiveness of sins, according to the riches of his grace' (Eph. 1:3-7).

2. 'Father, Give Me'

*W*e have concerned ourselves so far with a general introduction to the familiar parable of the prodigal son. Now we must go further into the story itself, the story of a young man's spiritual pilgrimage, of his sin and his repentance and his turning to God. We have already seen that this is the record of a man who represents publicans and sinners: that is to say, all those who are not to be classified as among the 'righteous,' the self-righteous, dependent upon themselves and their own obedience to the law for acceptance before God. While in one sense he is very plainly numbered among the lost sheep of the house of Israel, yet in another—and this is the great relevance of the parable to us Gentiles—he is also the universal sinner. He is Everyman in his trangression, need, and estrangement from God, in his wretchedness, misery, and hopelessness apart from the divine mercy.

His portrait is drawn for us with deep compassion, as one of the lost men and women of whom the world is full. Always there is in Christ's words a manifestation of the tenderness of his heart toward people like this. In the narrative of the woman taken in adultery, when her accusers, convicted at his rebuke by their own consciences, had drifted away, we are told that Jesus said to her: 'Woman, where are those thine accusers? hath no man condemned thee?' And when she answered, now full of shame and overwhelmed with repentance, 'No man, Lord,' he replied, 'Neither do I condemn thee: go, and sin no more' (John 8:10,11). To another such person, a woman 'which was a sinner,' he said, 'Thy sins are forgiven. Thy faith hath saved thee; go in peace' (Luke 7:48,50). When our Lord is dealing with the sin-sick, the world-weary, the bruised and broken, the penitent, however great their sin, there is no harshness, no condemnation; they know of that themselves and no longer need telling of it. Rather, there is acceptance, love tenderness, mercy, forgiveness: and then—thank God!—the joy and desire and power to lead a new and holy life.

I have already suggested that the prodigal stands for us all, that in a sense he is the universal sinner. Surely that is the case. Nothing about him strikes us as unusual or particularly significant. He does not seem to have been an extraordinary youth. As the story opens we are given no indication that he had been a difficult or delinquent boy. He is simply one of two sons in a good man's house. Though not so much as a word is said about the early years of his life, we have every reason to suppose that his childhood was a happy one; and it is plain, on the basis of what we know about his father, that his family background was sound and wholesome. Nothing is said about his mother. Christ's purpose was not to give us a full portrayal of the circumstances of the home and family life, but to point us to the sons in their relationship to the father.

What an extraordinary father that young man had! Is any

virtue lacking in him? He is obviously faithful, believing, patient, understanding, compassionate, and it is plain that he made every provision for the needs of his children. We are given to know very distinctly that whatever the shameful course of the prodigal's life after he left home and turned his back upon his father's love and restraining influence, the blame must rest altogether upon the young man, not upon the father. Again and again we must remind ourselves that the father represents God in his wisdom, love, and compassion. What a delineation of the heavenly Father! He is 'the Lord God, merciful and gracious, longsuffering, and abundant in goodness and truth, keeping mercy for thousands, forgiving iniquity and transgression and sin.' In the original description of God the words follow: 'and that will by no means clear the guilty' (Exod. 34:6,7). But, as we have said, it is not this aspect of truth which in the first instance is in view in the parable of the prodigal son. Here the whole accent is upon the other side: upon the mercy and grace and longsuffering and goodness of God who has himself made provision in his own Son for the recovery of sinners. I say, what a picture of God does not this set before us! And in what dark colours does not the subsequent behaviour of the young man appear!

The family background seems idyllic. It is hard to believe that so much misery could have flowed forth from such a relationship. And yet the parable has to do with the *prodigal* son. He was a prodigal. He sinned grievously against his father. Against all his privileges and opportunities as well, to be sure; but sin is never impersonal. It does not exist apart from persons; apart, in the highest, or rather deepest, sense from *the* Person. It is not a thing to which we can point as outside ourselves and which we can analyze neutrally from every one of its many facets, as a scientist does his specimen. We cannot speak abstractly about sin as though it were something with which we personally had nothing to do and which had invaded us from without. It is, on the contrary, intensely personal in all its manifestations. 'How then can I do this great wickedness, and sin *against God?*' (Gen. 39:9). That is the essence of sin. It is committed by persons, by created beings, beings moreover created in the image and likeness of God—an animal cannot sin!—and it is committed ultimately, not merely against other created persons, but against none other than God! Sin is done by persons against the divine Person: it is an assault upon the Being of God.

That the young man in the parable was a sinner it is impossible to deny. The whole story concerns just that fact. But where did the fault lie? The blame is not to be attributed to the father. Very often in our modern world the later misconduct of children is explained in terms of some parental failure, of some physical or moral neglect on the part of father and mother. Certainly the responsibility which rests upon parents for the forming of their children's lives is a tremendous one and can never be taken lightly. That which is neglected in youth it is difficult, if not impossible, to remedy afterwards, apart from the sovereign intervention of God. If children are not taught the truths of the Scriptures, are not trained in the way they should go, are not instructed in right and wrong, are not pointed to Christ, parents have very much to blame themselves when in later life the inevitable results of failure become evident.

But it is by no means possible to argue back from a life wrecked by sin to parental blame, and to say that because a son or daughter comes to lead a life of wickedness, therefore the parents *must* certainly have been at fault. Who of us is sufficient for these things? It is, after all, only the grace of God that brings any to Christ and spares any a life of folly and ruin. Some godly and faithful parents have had wretched children, for the wreckage of whose lives they were not responsible. That, the instance of the prodigal son also makes clear.

It has also to be said, as we look for the cause of this young man's going astray, that his sin, in the first instance, was not that he wasted his substance with riotous living. That was bad enough, but to speak of it is to concentrate on symptoms, rather than upon the root of the evil. His trouble was not essentially his misconduct, his individual acts of disobedience, bad as they were in themselves; rather, it was his *heart.* He had a heart, a nature, a being of corruption and sin and rebellion against God. That was his trouble. That is *the* universal trouble: 'The heart is deceitful above all things, and desperately wicked: who can know it?' (Jer. 17:9).

Here, then, is the point at which the prodigal's sin began. But the story admits of being analyzed further in this respect. His sin led to a condition of estrangement between the son and his father, and that estrangement was in clearly discernible stages.

First of all the young man became *dissatisfied with his father and with his father's house.* 'Give me,' he said, 'the portion of goods that falleth to me.' I do not suppose that this appalling and unnatural request was born in a moment's discontent. Such things almost never are! Rather, this demand for the inheritance that should have come to him after his father's death must have been preceded by a long period of gradually increasing desire to be free of restraint, to do as he pleased, and to have the means for indulging himself. No two people are exactly alike. And while one can stay at home and live in the relationship of a son to his father and mother, dependent upon them, willing to submit himself to the rules and regulations of a house that is not his own and over which he is not master, another chafes at such restrictions, longing instead to be lord of his own life and master of his own destiny. It is, of course, quite natural that at a certain age children go their own way. Dependence upon parents when continued too long can have sad results in the end. Those fathers and mothers who fail to understand this, and who attempt to subject their children, even when they have reached adulthood, to the same relationship that obtained when the children were small, make a very grave mistake. The child treated in this fashion will either be robbed of his or her individuality and fail to develop into the adulthood to which one ought to aspire, or the stage will have been set for an explosion, a tragic disruption of family ties, and a breaking of the unity and bonds of sympathy which should unite parents and children together. But it is not the normal desire for independence that we observe in the prodigal. His father was not over-possessive or bent upon subjecting his son to his own whims and desires. There is no evidence here that the father exercised a repressive authority over the son. The reverse is rather the case. No word of rebuke escapes the father's lips. He does not show anger at the son's unnatural request. It is in no sense true of him that, whether consciously or unconsciously, he wants to deprive the son of his own proper individuality and initiative. Nothing is wrong here with the father. It is only the son who is at fault.

That request of his, that desire for his inheritance, the means with which to make his own way in the world, amounts indeed to a declaration of spiritual independence. What he wants, what he will have, is to be free, not of his father's tyranny, for there was none, but of his father's testimony and example and holy life. He had had enough of life in a believing, faithful family circle. He chafed under dependence, under his filial position, and wanted to be out from under the weight, as it seemed to him, of the duties, obediences, and constraints which his situation entailed. It is the old story all over again, insofar as it can be repeated, of man's first rebellion against God at the very beginning of history. 'Yea, hath God said, Ye shall not eat of every tree of the garden? And the woman said unto the serpent, We may eat of the fruit of the trees of the garden: but of the fruit of the tree which is in the midst of the garden, God hath said, Ye shall not eat of it, neither shall ye touch it, lest ye die. And the serpent said unto the woman, Ye shall not surely die: for God doth know that in the day ye eat thereof, then your eyes shall be opened, and ye shall be as gods, knowing good and evil' (Gen. 3:1-5). I hardly need say that the prodigal did not occupy Adam's position, for he was heir to Adam's guilt and Adam's corrupt nature. But the root of the desire within him was the same. 'Ye shall be as gods, knowing good and evil.' That was what he wished: to be as a god, to know good and evil for himself, to serve his own interests, to throw off the restraints of faith and godliness, to be the director of his own fortunes and the satisfier of his own desires. 'Give me,' he said, 'give me the portion of goods that falleth to me.'

But is this not the very picture of sin and of the sinner? That surely is the essence of the thing: pride, to want one's own way, to live for oneself, to be free of external authority, to blot out the knowledge of the true and living God and instead to place oneself upon the throne that belongs only to him? It is of this that the Apostle Paul speaks when he says: 'When they knew God, they glorified him not as God, neither were thankful; but became vain in their imaginations, and their foolish heart was darkened. Professing themselves to be wise, they became fools, and changed the glory of the uncorruptible God into an image made like to corruptible man, and to birds, and fourfooted beasts, and creeping things' (Rom. 1:21-23). The black night of human ignorance, misery, and wretchedness begins at just this point: the declaration of independence from God. Horatius Bonar has captured something of what this means in the words:

> I was a wand'ring sheep,
> I did not love the fold;
> I did not love my Shepherd's voice,
> I would not be controlled.
> I was a wayward child,
> I did not love my home;
> I did not love my Father's voice,
> I loved afar to roam.

There it is! The home, the fold, the father's love, his good influences, his tenderness, compassion, wisdom, and grace mean nothing to us. We do not understand them. We cannot understand them as we are in ourselves. The whole bent of our natures is in another direction. It is not goodness we desire, or divine love, but our own way, even if it involves our going astray. Of course we do not think of ourselves as positively sinful, but as exercising what is our 'right.'

I remember a sad interview I once had with a young couple in which this came clearly to light. The boy had already turned his back upon two wives, and for no good reason divorced them. Now he presented himself to me with his prospective third bride to ask that I perform the marriage ceremony. When I spoke to him of the sinfulness of unwarranted divorce and reminded him of the need for repentance and humiliation before God, pointing out to him at the same time the unlawfulness of the marriage the two of them had in view, his response was that they had a 'right' to happiness. No man has a 'right' to what he may choose to call 'happiness', if happiness by which he sets such great store involves disobedience to the commandments of God. There is no such thing as a human 'right' over against God. And when a man makes that demand and insists upon having his own way—the divine law and the will of God notwithstanding, whether in marriage, or in business, or in personal relationships, or in any area of thought or conduct— he has placed himself thereby squarely upon the ground occupied by the prodigal son in Jesus' parable. He has declared that what matters is his freedom, his liberty to do what he pleases, so long as he derives satisfaction for himself. He believes that he knows best what he ought to do, that no power external to himself has the prerogative of laying down lines of conduct to guide his behavior. He is a free agent, and has the 'right,' the sovereign, untrammelled right, to do as he will. 'Ye shall be as gods.' 'Give me the portion of goods that falleth to me.'

But the parable's account of the prodigal's conduct does not stop with his dissatisfaction over his father's house and his declaration of independence. There follows another stage in his rebellion and estrangement. He also determined *to leave his father and his father's house.* He said to his father, 'Father, give me the portion of goods that falleth to me. And he divided unto them his living. And not many days after the younger son gathered all together, and took his journey into a far country' (Luke 15:12,13).

This second stage of his alienation from his father and his father's love took the form of his actively turning his back upon his home and living far away from the father, as far away as ever he could get. Once he decided to free himself from the uncomfortable and binding ties which restricted his liberty to do as he pleased, there could not be too much distance between himself and what he was no longer able to regard as the home of his soul. There is thus very evidently a progression in his descent into evil. Sin is a thirsty and demanding thing. When a man has made up his mind to do wrong, there can be no stopping with the initial sinful act. The exhilaration of freedom, the thrill of doing what one will, the apparent satisfaction of being the master of one's own fate, is not something in which a man can rest content with a single act, or even two or three. One step leads to another. One transgression produces a second and a third, and then an endless succession of transgressions which can only eventuate in ruin at last. We forget sometimes, at our convenience, the fact that sin, too, has its lusts, lusts which nothing but total abandonment—the utter devastation of character, its complete deprivation of honor, integrity, goodness, and truth—will assuage.

This is, of course, not something that one can make convincing to a person already well along on the road to destruction. He is in no condition to be persuaded of anything, as long as he is intent upon having his own way. A teachable and receptive spirit he does not know. Anyone, whether heading in the direction of open moral depravity, or ruthlessly climbing the ladder to ultimate success in some business enterprise without a thought for those he has injured or destroyed along the way, or simply living a self-ish, self-centered, godless, Christless life, is quite sure that he knows better what he needs and what his life is all about than those whose voices seek to put him in mind once again of the Father, the Father's love, and the Father's house. And yet, heedless as such persons may be—as perhaps *you* may be—this truth of the hungry, thirsty, voracious charac-ter of evil is a truth we need to have constantly set before us.

Obviously, no one sets out to destroy his body or to cor-rupt his soul; no one with his wits about him is bent upon self-destruction in the pursuit of the unlawful and the forbidden—forbidden, that is, by God. The Scriptures tell us time and again, however, that sin in and of itself bears just this fruit. In fact, a part of the judgment of God upon sin is its self-multiplying quality. In his great indictment of the peoples of the world for their ungodliness the Apostle Paul asserts that on this account 'God also gave them up to uncleanness through the lusts of their own hearts, to dis-honour their own bodies between themselves; who changed the truth of God into a lie, and worshipped the creature more than the Creator, who is blessed for ever.' Then he repeats: 'For this cause *God gave them up* unto vile affec-tions.' And once again in this passage, for the third time, he declares: 'And even as they did not like to retain God in their knowledge, *God gave them over* to a reprobate mind, to do those things which are not convenient; being filled with all unrighteousness, fornication, wickedness, covetous-ness, maliciousness; full of envy, murder, debate, deceit, malignity; whisperers, backbiters, haters of God, despiteful, proud, boasters, inventors of evil things, disobedient to parents, without understanding, covenant-breakers, without natural affection, implacable, unmerciful' (Rom. 1:24ff.). No one means to end in this way, but that is what happens when a man declares his independence of God and determines to serve himself, rather than the Creator. 'And not many days after the younger son . . . took his journey into a far country.'

But the prodigal did more than that. The first sign of his estrangement from the father was his request for the inheritance that would have been his upon his father's death. To act rightly he should have waited till in the normal course of life this would have come to him. But somehow he could not. It is a repulsive thing, this demanding as of right what was not his. Now and again one hears of instances similar to this, and always the effect upon us must be that there is something unnatural about it, that the fires of affection within a family must be burning very low, that an action which anticipates the death of a parent and which by its very nature cannot but severely wound the heart of a father or mother must be motivated by a near total break-down of communication, of respect, of love. To ask a father's help in time of some pressing need is one thing; to demand one's inheritance in advance quite another. But it is just this which the young man did, so insensitive, so completely without regard for the father's feelings and love had he become.

Now, independent of home, at a great distance, as he thought, from all restraining influence, in that far country for which he so long had earnestly yearned, there he *wasted his substance with riotous living.'*

It is called 'his substance.' And in a sense it was that. The father had made it over to him, and he could legally use it quite as he pleased. Yet in another and higher sense that substance was not his. Ultimately it did not belong to him. He could not claim the right to dispose of it according to his own whim and desire. The father lived still. And the substance, the wealth and possessions he had successfully demanded, all that he had was the father's, not the prodigal son's. Hence, whatever use he made of it, however he spent it, wherever he squandered it, even in that far country, for all that he was yet accountable to the one to whom it continued to belong.

There is here a very disquieting truth, and one which we cannot allow to escape us. For the whole history of man apart from God, alienated from him, has been in great measure an attempt to forget that he is not his own, that he belongs to the Creator, and that, whatever he has and whatever he is, even whatever he may hope to become, he is not a free agent answerable to no one but himself, but ultimately and finally to God. It was just this that the first man, Adam, forgot when he did what God had commanded him not to do and ate of the forbidden fruit. Throughout the Old Testament we read of instance after instance when Israel forgot this also and had to be sharply rebuked by the prophets and humbled before the Lord. In your own life, and in the line of conduct you have followed, you have forgotten it, too. But remember that your mind, your body, your talents, your position, your family, the things you appear to possess, are all God's at last, and only entrusted to your keeping for a time. What a dreadful thing it is to waste one's substance—substance that is really not one's own at all, but God's—in riotous living, and then to have to give an accounting in the end for the squandering of it, and to have nothing to say! I say, what a dreadful thing it is for a man, a woman, a community, a society, a whole civilization, to use carelessly and heedlessly, and with no eye to the consequences, all that God has given only in charge, and to stand naked, speechless, condemned at last.

A declaration of spiritual independence, dissatisfaction with the fellowship of the father, estrangement from the father in a far country, the wasting of the father's substance in careless and riotous living: these describe the experience of man the sinner. No wonder, then, the wretchedness and misery, the deep unhappiness and dissatisfaction which he finds on all sides! He is a prodigal, a son of the father, a product of the Creator's hand, but he is lost. And that lostness of his can never, never change, though it may be possible for him now and again to forget the relationship which once was, the joy upon which he turned his back, and the terrible debt under which he lives: I say, that lostness of his can never, never change until, in the love and compassion and tenderness of God, the prodigal, humbled, empty, broken, is welcomed home again by the Father's boundless mercy in the only Saviour of sinners.

> *Weary of earth, and laden with my sin,*
> *I look at heav'n and long to enter in;*
> *But there no evil thing may find a home;*
> *And yet I hear a voice that bids me 'Come!'*
>
> *So vile I am, how dare I hope to stand*
> *In the pure glory of that holy land?*
> *Before the whiteness of that throne appear?*
> *Yet there are hands stretched out to draw me near.*

The while I fain would tread the heav'nly way,
Evil is ever with me day by day;
Yet on mine ears the gracious tidings fall,
'Repent, confess, thou shalt be loosed from all!'

It is the voice of Jesus that I hear;
His are the hands stretched out to draw me near,
And his the blood that can for all atone,
And set me faultless there before the throne.

(Samuel J. Stone)

3. 'He Began To Be in Want'

The picture drawn for us by the Lord Jesus Christ at which we have begun to look is thus far an altogether sad one. And yet, from the young man's point of view, this opportunity to make his fortune, to use his life as it suited him, was very likely not sad at all. He aimed at pleasure, not misery, and on this account the satisfactions available to him in his father's house he found by no means sufficient.

We see him setting out gaily, therefore, with great hopes to make his fortune and way in the world. There was no thought in his mind of rejected privileges, of thwarted hopes, of neglected opportunities, of broken promises. He only had time now for the enjoyment which was in prospect for him, the pleasures which were now within his grasp. Nothing could keep him back from trying his hand at the business of living according to his own will and determination. He was his own master, the captain and custodian of his own soul. Surely one feels something of the exhilaration, the sense of expectancy, which must have captivated his whole being as he turned away from that constricting, now rejected home in which he had been brought up!

But we must follow the son in his subsequent course of life. Now he had money: he could do as he pleased. And he did! That his money had come from his father made no difference to him. All that mattered was what he could buy, and he literally threw it away for momentary satisfaction and pleasure.

It bought him friends. And what friends they were! As long as the source of supply held out, they remained faithful to him, enjoying what he could give them and himself.

It bought him love, or at any rate, what he thought of as 'love.' The elder brother said later on, when the prodigal returned home, that he had devoured the father's living with prostitutes. There is no reason to doubt that this was the case. But he discovered, when the money was gone, that there was no love in them at all. So great was his confusion, a confusion he shares with countless others, that he identified passion with love and failed to understand any of the purer, nobler emotions and feelings which he had once seen daily in the person of his own father. And the lust, which he fancied was love, when the money was gone with which to purchase it, even that had turned to ashes in his mouth and was no longer available to him.

It bought him forgetfulness of home and his father. All the while that he could live carelessly, indulgently, covering over the promptings of his conscience with an avalanche of pleasure, his mind was distracted from what he had left behind him. He had no thought of his father and his father's hopes and his father's love. What he wanted to put out of his mind, he managed successfully to forget.

It bought him himself, or what he conceived to be himself. At home self-expression had been impossible. He was a son, a younger son at that, in the house of another, even if his own father. And it was a godly house, a house of love and of compassion and of joy, to be sure, but also a house of discipline and of principle and of obedience, where a fellow with his talent and his inclination had no chance in the world of being what he felt within him he was able to become. But in that far country a man could develop and be himself and grow into the kind of person he wanted to be. There he could exercise his own right to be an individual human being, his own right to personal happiness. And he did so, or was foolish enough to suppose that he did so, until the money was gone that enabled him to buy what he thought of as self-expression, the prerogative of being himself, and then he quickly discovered the illusoriness of what he had achieved. It vanished away into nothing.

So he wasted his substance with riotous living. He bought all he could buy with money. He spent his days in the pursuit of himself, his own satisfactions and pleasures, he did what he had always wanted to do, until that substance of his or of his father's, was all gone, and, Jesus tells us, 'he began to be in want.' How could it have gone so quickly? He had had enough for many a long day. Where did it go? Why was it not enough to sustain him in his mode of life? But it was gone. It was all gone. He had nothing! And then, to compound the difficulty, a great famine arose in that far country of his, which he had desired so earnestly and to which he had given himself so whole-heartedly, and he felt hunger. For the first time in his life he was actually hungry, without food, without bread enough to eat. And he began to understand want: deep, genuine want of food and drink, of the first necessities of life. There is a great deal in those few simple words: 'And when he had spent all, there arose a mighty famine in that land; and he began to be in want' (v. 14).

It is at this point when the young man becomes aware of his deep distress that there is a sense in which we can say that he also becomes a singularly happy man. Not everyone in a 'far country' reaches the point of being in want. Indeed, I believe it is true to say that a vast number never become aware of their wretched and miserable condition. They, like the prodigal, have spent themselves and all that they have in their own interests; they have given their time to the things that have no ultimate reality and must inevitably perish at last; but they are not brought up sharply, or made to be aware of the true nature of their situation. There may be a vague, indistinct consciousness that something is amiss, that they have not succeeded in their drive toward self-fulfilment. But that is all. And they die in the state in which they have lived, forever—and how inexpressibly sad is that word!—forever cut off from the only source of true joy and lasting satisfaction. 'He began to be in want.' That awareness of lacking something is the initial step in any man's pilgrimage to God.

We have come to the first stage in the spiritual pilgrimage of the prodigal son, the first positive indication of his returning to the father's house. This is described in verse 14, words which follow hard upon the heels of those which tell us of the degree to which the young man fell away from everything he had ever heard or learned from his father: 'And when he had spent all, there arose a mighty famine in that land; and he began to be in want.' The prodigal has come to an end of sinning. He begins to be aware of his deep distress and of the wretchedness of the position in which he finds himself. He is in want!

Now we follow the story a step further and discover that

there is an end to sinning because it affords no ultimate satisfaction. That, surely, is very evident from what the Lord Jesus Christ tells us here. What is the issue of that period of self-indulgence, that wasting of his substance in riotous living, that devouring of his father's goods with prostitutes and sinners? 'He began to be in want. And he went and joined himself to a citizen of that country; and he sent him into his fields to feed swine. And he would fain have filled his belly with the husks that the swine did eat: and no man gave unto him' (vv. 14-16).

Mind you, when I say that there is an end to sinning because it affords no ultimate satisfaction, I am not suggesting that there is no kind of satisfaction in sin. One would have to be very ignorant and blind indeed to think anything of the sort! Sin does have its pleasures. Human nature is most perverse in itself, and quite capable of following a line of action simply because that line of action is forbidden. Something in us is determined to do what we know we ought not to do precisely because we know we ought not to do it. The Apostle Paul was describing something of the kind when he said: 'For the good that I would I do not: but the evil which I would not, that I do' (Rom. 7:19). Hence there is a sense in which no pleasure or satisfaction need be involved in order for us to disobey. The very sinfulness of sin, its forbiddenness, its having been proscribed and prohibited, is enough to induce us to commit it. No doubt children provide a graphic illustration of this kind of thing. The making of rules to govern their behavior is itself a ground for breaking them. The sensation of doing something unlawful, something we know is wrong, is itself even pleasureable in a measure, so far have we fallen from the state in which God created us. But beyond all that, it is foolish to deny that there may be pleasure in sinning. Of course there may!

The thief who is successful in taking from others what is not his satisfies his greed. He covets what belongs to someone else, and manages to contrive a way to appropriate it for himself. A bold and ruthless man, craving power in the economic structures of a country, may plan and scheme and gamble, and, often ruthlessly riding roughshod over others to attain his end, finds pleasure in manipulating those whom he has managed to get within his grasp. The adulterer pursues his lusts in the interests of temporary gratification, even though he himself may be quite aware of the fleeting nature of the pleasure he achieves for himself. The drunkard can be conscious of the fact that he is destroying both his mind and his body by his addiction to drink, and yet judge that the pleasure he derives from the oblivion of his drunkenness is worth the risk: it gives him some satisfaction despite the inevitable consequences.

But it is not only such sins that yield a certain measure of satisfaction. The so-called 'respectable sins' have their pleasureable sensations, too. While they would be the last to admit it, the self-righteous experience a great deal of pleasure from their superiority—their moral and perhaps even religious superiority—above others. And the same thing is true of pride—that feeling of accomplishment, of having raised oneself by one's own efforts, of being more able because more successful in this or that respect than others. The gratification King Nebuchadnezzar derived from his own achievements may be seen in the boasting words which brought about his humiliation before God: 'Is not this great Babylon, that I have built for the house of the kingdom by the might of my power, and for the honour of my majesty?'

(Dan. 4:30). There was certainly enjoyment and pleasure in revelling in that tremendous accomplishment!

Sin is not all of the same kind. It is not all of a single variety. Too often people are ready to think that only those forms of behavior are sinful which respectable men and women universally condemn. But a man may easily condemn conduct that is obviously sinful, and yet himself be guilty of finding gratification in things which are just as reprehensible before God as greed or lust or murder.

The point is, however, that one must ask the question: What is there in all this at last? Where do carelessness, unrestraint, self-righteousness, pride, all lead in the end? 'A wonderful and horrible thing is committed in the land: The prophets prophesy falsely, and the priests bear rule by their means, and my people love to have it so; and'—this, mark well, is the climax and the utterly essential inquiry— 'what will ye do in the end thereof?' (Jer. 5:30,31).

I began by saying, not that there is no satisfaction in sinning, but that there is no ultimate satisfaction in it. The prodigal enjoyed himself while his money lasted, and in one way it lasted far too long for his own good; but when the money had been used up and there was no more, when his purse was empty in that far country of his, then he discovered that what he had enjoyed was only temporary, and that its end was emptiness, frustration, unhappiness.

This failure of sin to give satisfaction has many causes. *For one thing, the ability which it has to interest us quickly runs out.* In fact, this is one of the characteristic features of life without God. An unbelieving life is a hungry, thirsty life, always demanding more. Desire may be satisfied by this or that for the time being, but the old feeling of restlessness and unease soon returns, and a man or woman finds it necessary to turn elsewhere, perhaps to still worse forms of the same sin, or to new sins altogether. But again, interest pales and pleasure lessens, for there is no final satisfaction in sin.

It is also true of sin that its power to convey pleasure may be quickly dissipated. All the 'happiness' of a particular form of behavior can soon turn to gall and bitterness in the very mouth of one who has enjoyed it. Of course, habit is strong; it is a difficult thing to break off what one has been doing, even long after the enchantment of it has disappeared. But the continued existence of the habit by no means indicates that the person in its grip finds any satisfaction in what he is doing.

Once again, and now on a higher plane, a man cannot find ultimate fulfilment and contentment in sin, because he is not a beast—not as the 'horse, or as the mule, which have no understanding' (Ps. 32:9). In this parable we must never forget that under the figure of a hungry and thirsty prodigal, who has spent all he had on a life of careless indulgence, the Lord is speaking of a sinful man separated from *his* God. The prodigal is still a *son,* and he cannot rest in a life cut off from his father. Just so is it with every man who attempts to live without God. He was made for better things. He is not merely body, but also soul. He was created in the image of God. How then can he be satisfied to live as though he were a mindless, soulless animal which has no conscience and was never created for fellowship with God? When one pauses to reflect on the matter, it becomes clear that for man, made as he was for another dimension of experience, designed for another purpose, there can be no lasting enjoyment or happiness in a life like that of the prodigal son.

We have left our Father and our Father's house; we live in

alienation and estrangement from him. But that does not mean that nothing remains of the longing God placed within us and that our consciences have been utterly destroyed. We *know* there is something better. There is still within us a residual awareness of other, higher things. Of course there is! And on that account a life centered on oneself and one's own interests and desires, a life lived in wilful, stubborn defiance of God and his will, is a poor, shoddy substitute for what man was intended to be. 'And God said, Let us make man in our image, after our likeness; and let them have dominion over the fish of the sea, and over the fowl of the air, and over the cattle, and over all the earth, and over every creeping thing that creepeth upon the earth. So God created man in his own image, in the image of God created he him' (Gen. 1:26,27). It was with that in mind, and to that end, that God made us. How then can sin satisfy us at last?

Once more, in the presence of the grave realities of life, and in the face of the death and judgment which confront us all without any single exception, *we begin to see our disobedience and our estrangement from our Father and from our Father's house in their true significance*. It were one thing if life continued forever, uninterrupted by the inevitableness of decay and death; but that is not the case. It is not the case for you. It may seem to you that there is nothing more worth doing than to live for yourself, whatever form that self-centered existence of yours may take, whether respectable or not; but I tell you that this is a terrible delusion on your part. 'For the wages of sin is death' (Rom. 6:23). There is an end to sinning, because it can yield no ultimate satisfaction. Only the Lord Jesus Christ can do that!

We have observed that the prodigal began to be in want, was possessed of a dawning awareness of his deep distress and wretchedness, because there is no ultimate satisfaction in sin. That leads us to the next stage in our analysis. Not only is there an end to sinning because it affords no ultimate satisfaction, but also *because it can only induce spiritual starvation*.

A man cannot live by bread alone. God 'humbled thee,' Moses told the twelve tribes of Israel, 'and suffered thee to hunger, and fed thee with manna, which thou knewest not, neither did thy fathers know; that he might make thee know that man doth not live by bread only, but by every word that proceedeth out of the mouth of the Lord doth man live' (Deut. 8:3). These words were used by the Lord Jesus Christ to overthrow the temptation of the devil (Matt. 4:4), and their truth is constant. Still less can a man live by selfishness and pleasure alone. And least of all can he live without God, as though he were alone on this planet, answerable only to himself, or at most to his fellow-men. This was what the prodigal had to be brought to see.

'And when he had spent all, there arose a mighty famine in that land; and he began to be in want. And he went and joined himself to a citizen of that country, and he sent him into his fields to feed swine. And he would fain have filled his belly with the husks that the swine did eat; and no man gave unto him.' To this miserable condition was the proud, self-sufficient young man reduced who only shortly before had demanded his inheritance and then set out to make his way in the great world. He thought the supply endless; he fancied himself able to live freely and luxuriously in whatever style he chose. But now the source of supply had dried up. The money was gone. And he lacked even bread.

Now, a person in this position may try many alternatives instead of turning to God. The prodigal did that at first. 'He went and joined himself to a citizen of that country; and he sent him into his fields to feed swine.' That was his attempt at self-help, at finding his own way out of the predicament into which he had brought himself. A man may try any number of things.

Some cast themselves into still more violent forms of sin. They use the self-multiplying quality of sin as a kind of mental and spiritual narcotic. It may drown the voices of conscience and of God for a time, and in that sense be a temporarily successful remedy. But gradually one is sucked deeper and deeper into the morass of hopelessness and despair, and at last it becomes clear that there is something suicidal about that kind of approach to the problem of sin. To continue in that path would be to destroy oneself.

Others take the way of moral reform. They attempt to remedy their own ailments, to clean up their own lives, to discontinue their former habits, to alter their mode and style of life. And some, it must be said, are successful in halting their downward course, in radically improving their moral position. Self-reformation is by no means unknown. Yet however worthy in itself, such action does nothing to change the emaciated condition of our spiritual frame, or to take away the barrier that has arisen between us and the God who made us.

Still others may go the way of false religion. We live in a day in which many boast of their tolerance, and assume that all kinds of religion are of similar value. The prevalent notion in many quarters is that it matters little what a person believes, so long as he believes it sincerely and does his best to live in accordance with it. But upon the basis of what

God has revealed to us in his Word, a Christian must utterly repudiate any such theory. To be sure, the adherents of other religious faiths may be perfectly sincere. They may also live moral and peaceable lives, do good to their neighbors, engage in philanthropy, take an active part in community life, and be highly respectable. But these things have no necessary relationship to the truth of what they profess. Certainly a Christian so-called, who does not show his faith in his manner of life, is really no Christian at all. But a non-Christian, no matter what his manner of life, still professes and believes a lie. And there can be no help, no salvation, no forgiveness, no firm basis for the erecting of a life, in a lie. One is still in a starving position, still longing for the husks that the swine did eat, still in that far country. Try as he will, until a man returns to the father's house he can only grow weaker still, more and more lost in the desperate loneliness and eternal isolation of the consuming spiritual cancer which is sin.

But remember that this young man's growing awareness of want is all part of the sovereign plan of God. He is not yet really conscious of his true condition, but that consciousness is beginning to dawn, and it is the Father who has been at work in bringing about this. For, as we said at the outset, the Father in Christ's story is not merely a human father who beyond a certain point is incapable of being any help. He is God, and he will save! You see, thus, that it is God's hand which is to be discerned in the prodigal's frustration and dissatisfaction and spiritual hunger, that hand which is stretched out still, in mercy and in grace, through all the famine and want and loneliness of the far country. It reaches across endless distances, bridges vast chasms, and encompasses even the spiritually destitute, the emaciated, the dead in trespasses and sins! What a great thing it is to know of that extended hand, of that pursuing love, of that boundless, infinite compassion, of which the Apostle Paul so beautifully speaks when he says: 'God commendeth his love toward us, in that, while we were yet sinners, Christ died for us' (Rom. 5:8)!

It is indeed the compassion of God, the Father, which gives that erring, prodigal son of his no peace or rest or contentment away from his home, but effectively shuts him up to the one avenue by which at last he may return again from that far country of wasted substance and riotous living to the Father's house and to the Father's love. The whole of salvation, every step in the spiritual pilgrimage of any person, is a matter of the divine grace. There is nothing of man in it. Left to himself the prodigal would certainly have died far from home, in the barren field where he longed for husks, and no man gave to him. But he was never alone. The Father's everlasting love had never abandoned him. And the first step—that beginning to be in want, that dissatisfaction with life as he knew and led it—was itself a token of the triumphantly saving grace of the heavenly Father.

4. 'When He Came to Himself'!

*W*e go on now to the next phase in the spiritual history of the prodigal son in Jesus' great parable. So far we have seen the young man in want, having discovered that there is an end to sinning, and that one can find no ultimate satisfaction but only spiritual starvation and death in a life separated from God. It was a feeble step, that sensation of want, but it was a step in the right direction. It represented a change in his mind, a shifting in his point of view, and it had validity because it came from his father: it was an effect of his father's love. We can now follow him further and see him begin to turn more and more away from that life of abandonment and sin to the house he had left far behind him.

'And when he came to himself, he said, How many hired servants of my father's have bread enough and to spare, and I perish with hunger!' (v. 17). Take especial note of these words: 'And when he came to himself.' What volumes they speak! 'He came *to himself.*' That is, his mind was restored to him and began to become sound and healthy once again. 'For God hath not given us the spirit of fear,' says the Apostle Paul; 'but of power, and of love, and of a sound mind' (2 Tim. 1:7).

An incident in the Old Testament graphically illustrates this same truth. Nebuchadnezzar, the great king of Babylon, was brought to his knees before God for his towering pride. As a judgment his soundness of mind was taken from him, we are told, and he was driven from men. He had to live with the beasts of the field and eat grass as the oxen, until seven times passed over him and he came to know that the most High rules in the kingdom of men, giving it to whomsoever he will. When that time came, 'at the end of the days'—it is the king himself who tells us of his own experience—'I Nebuchadnezzar lifted up mine eyes unto heaven, and mine understanding returned to me, and I blessed the most High, and I praised and honoured Him that liveth forever, whose dominion is an everlasting dominion, and his kingdom is from generation to generation . . . all whose works are truth, and his ways judgment: and those that walk in pride he is able to abase' (Dan. 4:34,37).

Here, then, we observe that when the prodigal comes to a dawning consciousness of his sin and of his alienation from the father he begins at long last to recover soundness of mind.

Consider, first of all, *that the prodigal reveals here a grasp of his true spiritual condition.* This is implied, surely, in the words: 'when he came to himself.' There is a difference which it is necessary for us to understand between a general *sense* of sin, and a *conviction* of sin. The former—a sense of personal inadequacy—is very nearly universal, and I do not doubt but that the prodigal himself, well taught as he was in the truths of the Old Testament, even in the darkest days of his profligacy and self-indulgence would have admitted to being a sinner in this meaning of the word. He had some measure of an understanding of human sinfulness, a sense of being a sinner. It is interesting to watch for the reactions people display when asked the question: Are you a sinner? Nearly always the answer will be: Yes, certainly; everyone is a sinner. The point is, of course, that people who answer in this way very likely have a sense of sin, a consciousness of not being as they ought to be and of living in some degree of disobedience to God, but it is only that, and tempered at the same time by the knowledge that after all they share this condition with every other man, woman, and child in the world. What is more, this common sense of sin can frequently lead to the need for a 'religious faith'; it can motivate religious enterprise and be a basic driving force for the many and sometimes quite extraordinary accomplishments of men and women. The awareness of being flawed and imperfect, of being somewhat less than one ought to be, is almost universal. And it makes people think of God in a general sense and give a kind of worship to him.

A true conviction of sin is something very different. Many indeed have a sense of sin, but they are far fewer who understand what it is to be under *conviction* of sin. Those with only a superficial grasp of the sinfulness of mankind, and of their own hearts, have no true knowledge of conviction. They are not prepared to humble themselves before God, nor do they feel the necessity to use the only words which are appropriate to us, 'God be merciful to me a sinner' (Luke 18:13).

But what is this Christian thing, this conviction of sin, this recognition of one's true spiritual condition which is reflected in the prodigal's experience by the words, 'and when he came to himself'? After asking the question, 'How many things is it necessary for thee to know, that thou mayest live and die happily?' the old Heidelberg Catechism gives the answer: 'Three things: First, the greatness of my sin and misery. Second, how I am redeemed from all my sin and misery. Third, how I am to be thankful to God for such redemption' (Ques. 2). The crucial consideration for our purposes here is, of course, the first. I must know the greatness of my sin and misery: that is conviction of sin. And the Westminster Confession of Faith teaches the same fundamental doctrine. 'Repentance unto life is an evangelical grace, the doctrine whereof is to be preached by every minister of the gospel, as well as that of faith in Christ. By it a sinner, out of the sight and sense, not only of the danger, but also of the filthiness and odiousness of his sins, as contrary to the holy nature and righteous law of God, and upon the apprehension of his mercy in Christ to such as are penitent, so grieves for, and hates his sins, as to turn from them all unto God, purposing and endeavoring to walk with him in all the ways of his commandments' (XV/1,2).

The words which a repenting prodigal may use are not always the same, but the effect is indeed the same. The basic truth is that it is not enough to be vaguely aware that we are not quite what we ought to be. That sort of thing is universal, as we have seen, and not necessarily Christian. Certainly it is not enough to satisfy the demands of the gospel. Not, of course, as though a true conviction of sin were a kind of work on the part of the sinner in which he is to demonstrate that he takes seriously the fact of his alienation from God and his blameworthiness and his guilt. Hardly that! 'Not by works of righteousness which we have done, but according to his mercy he saved us' (Tit. 3:5). For this very conviction of sin, this utter abandonment of self and of one's own righteousness and of one's own pretensions and of one's own pride before God, this acknowledgement that one is naked and destitute and without hope in himself in the presence of the altogether Holy One, this also is of the Holy Spirit and in no sense at all the work of man the sinner.

Have you, I wonder, any experience at all of a conviction of sin? One of the great problems with much evangelical preaching and teaching is that it has been negligent at just this point. It has been supposed that when a person has something of a sense of sin, some degree of awareness that his spiritual condition is a serious one, when he has been brought by some means to a public recognition of this, then a work of grace has taken place and he has become a Christian. Such, however, is simply not the case. When God does a work he does it thoroughly. And while remorse and a superficial, unenduring sorrow for sin can be induced by merely human means, the conviction of sin which is a right understanding of the true nature of one's spiritual condition can come only from God. A man in the grip of conviction has been taught how great his sins and miseries are. He has come to understand what his position is—of guilt and of blameworthiness and of death—before the holiness and the justice of God!

I suppose that the prodigal always had a sense of sin. He was too well taught in his father's house not to have had that knowledge. We need not think that the young man was quite without any knowledge or awareness of the need for religious faith even when he was enjoying himself with abandon in the far country. The embezzler, the covetous, the adulterer, the self-righteous, the hater, the liar, these are not necessarily irreligious persons who are so far depraved as to have turned utterly away from a belief in God, and sin, and the need for salvation. Not at all! But only when he came to himself did the prodigal begin to reveal that he now had something more than a mere sense of sin, a mere awareness that something might possibly be wrong with him morally. Now there is a dawning conviction of sin. And this is the most hopeful thing in the world. The young man, sadly old now because of what he had done to himself, at last thought of his own past, of the degree of his guilt, of the love he had spurned, and of the depths to which he had sunk. These are genuine tokens that he had finally been awakened to the seriousness of his spiritual position. And you notice that his mind turns now to his father and his father's house.

I say that this whole matter of a conviction of sin is the most hopeful thing in the world. And I say so because it means that a man who has been convicted in this way is being drawn to God. When he discovers his own leanness and is overwhelmed by it, when he realizes that he has done all his wickedness and sin against God, when he perceives the verticalness, the Godwardness implicit in every act of sin—that it is committed ultimately not against others, not against oneself, but against God—there is evidence that the heavenly Father is at work in drawing the sinner to himself. And as that conviction of sin comes, you will discover it to be accompanied always, though by no means necessarily at once, by the sweet, enduring persuasion that there is forgiveness with the Lord, that he may be feared (Ps. 130:4).

But let us go on to a second observation in connection with this stage in the return of the prodigal to his father.

Consider, then, further *that the prodigal reveals a grasp of his remediless hopelessness left to himself and his own devices.* In that far country which he once had so eagerly desired to see and where he had been so sure he would be able to make his way in the world, he began to think of his father and his father's house and of what had been his when he lived there as a son. 'And when he came to himself, he said, How many hired servants of my father's have bread enough and to spare, and I perish with hunger!' (v. 17).

'I perish with hunger,' he cried. He knew now that he was dying. He had gone, you remember, to a farmer in that far country, willing to do any kind of work. And the lowliest job had been assigned to him, one that must have been utterly repulsive to a man with his background. Not only had he been possessed of great privilege as the son of a wealthy family, but he was also a Jew; and to him the work of feeding swine was in conflict with what he understood of the will of God. A pig was an unclean animal, and now here he was, destitute, and reduced to this to keep body and soul together. But even the feeding of swine was not enough. A great famine prevailed in that land; labor was cheap; no one felt any obligation to take pity on him. What he earned in his new occupation was such as to leave him starving still. He shortly became so desperate for food that, Jesus tells us, 'he would fain have filled his belly with the husks that the swine did eat: and no man gave unto him.' No wonder then that he said: 'I perish with hunger!'

The prodigal was dying, and he knew it. And what was more, he now had no way of doing anything about it. His money was gone, and with it his friends. But he had lost much more than a mere inheritance, and even that—which he had so earnestly coveted in the past—loomed less large in his mind than it once had done. You see, he had lost his innocence. That was gone with his riotous living. He had, so far as he knew, lost all human sympathy. 'And no man gave unto him.' He had lost his home. He had taken his journey into a far country, and now, everything had gone but thoughts, bare thoughts, of his father's house. He had for the time lost hope. He could reflect upon the past, but there is small comfort in that if it appears that there is no chance of recovery and restoration. Only gradually does he begin to think that perhaps he may secure a servant's place in the household in which he had once lived as a son. But for the time being there is only black depression; 'I perish with hunger.'

I said that he was dying. But this dying of his in the way of starvation is a picture, a symbol, of something far more profound. And that Christ intended us to see it as such is clear from some words which the father spoke after the prodigal had come home again. 'This my son,' he declared, 'was dead, and is alive again; he was lost, and is found' (v. 24). You see, the young man was beginning to realize something that the Scriptures are constantly concerned to teach us. The Apostle Paul declares in the second chapter of his Epistle to the Ephesians: 'And you hath he quickened, who were dead in trespasses and sins: wherein in time past ye walked according to the course of this world, according to the prince of the power of the air, the spirit that now worketh in the children of disobedience: among whom also we all had our conversation in times past in the lusts of our flesh, fulfilling the desires of the flesh and of the mind; and were by nature the children of wrath, even as others. But God, who is rich in mercy, for his great love wherewith he loved us, even when we were dead in sins, hath quickened us together with Christ' (vv. 1-5). 'And you he has made alive who were *dead* in trespasses and sins.' The meaning here is, of course, not that non-Christians are literally, physically dead in sin. If that were the case all hope would have to be abandoned. There would be no point in preaching the gospel. For while we yet live, even though we are spiritually dead, there is opportunity to hear the gospel and to believe it and to be saved. But man is in a condition of spiritual death. He is dead to God. He is dead in all his trespasses and sins. 'By one man sin entered into the world, and death by sin; and so death passed upon all men, for that all have sinned' (Rom. 5:12). These two things go together: a loss of hope and a sense of being dead to God. You see thus what I meant when I suggested that the prodigal in these words reveals a grasp of his remediless hopelessness left to himself and his own devices.

The question which engaged his mind must have been very much like that expressed by the Old Testament prophet Micah. 'Wherewith shall I come before the Lord, and bow myself before the high God? Shall I come before him with burnt offerings, with calves of a year old? Will the Lord be pleased with thousands of rams, or with ten thousands of rivers of oil? Shall I give my firstborn for my transgression, the fruit of my body for the sin of my soul?' (6:6,7). It will have struck you that the prophet is here asking himself: What can *I do* to please God? How shall I in my own strength appear before him? And this is a very natural thing. Micah knew better, certainly, as the context clearly indicates. But Micah understood the grace of God, as the prodigal did not at this stage, and as perhaps you do not at this stage. In a true conviction of sin, when God is dealing with the heart of man and the Holy Spirit is genuinely at work, the first thing that has to be learned—and it is inextricably bound up with an understanding of the truth that sin is committed *against* God—is that there is nothing, nothing whatsoever in the world, that I can do to merit or to earn the favor of God. Salvation is utterly and entirely of grace. Hope is born not of what I can contribute, but of resting only in the sufficient, the gloriously and eternally sufficient work of our Lord Jesus Christ on the cross.

I must point out that the prodigal is not alone in this sudden awareness of the fatal nature of his position. In many instances people are struck down just as this young man was. They go on step by step in a life of sin and disobedience and self-sufficiency, concentrating all their powers on the things that do not matter, but managing to hide from others their engrossment with selfishness and pride and evil; and so extraordinary is man in the structures of his mind and spirit that he is able to cover over all this even from himself. The faculty of self-justification is a colossal and potent one, and the lengths to which a man may go in this direction know almost no bounds at all. But then something happens. Perhaps his marriage falls apart. It may be that his children turn against him. Sometimes it happens that a secret sin, theft, drunkenness, immoral conduct, is exposed to the light of day. And when this comes about, when family and friends begin to see that what they had thought of a man had no basis in fact; that his reputation was quite different from his true character within; when a man sees the edifice of his life lying about his feet in ruins, then he may be filled with remorse, his conscience awakened, his mind possessed by a feeling of desperate hopelessness. What has come about appears to him then so completely without remedy, so unchangeable, so permanent, that he sees no way out.

Obviously enough, this kind of occurrence does not always have a good result. Hopelessness may lead to still more drastic behavior than was the case in the past. But on the other hand, as in the instance of the prodigal, this exposure may come to be seen, in the words of the Apostle Paul, as the goodness of God leading men to repentance (Rom. 2:4). Though what is done cannot ever be undone, yet the greatest and brightest and most glorious hope of all is in that very hopelessness which shuts men up to God: to the God who says, 'I have blotted out, as a thick cloud, thy transgressions, and, as a cloud, thy sins: return unto me; for I have redeemed thee' (Is. 44:22), and to the God of whom it is said: 'Who is a God like unto thee, that pardoneth iniquity, and passeth by the transgression of the remnant of his heritage? he retaineth not his anger for ever, because he delighteth in mercy. He will turn again, he will have compassion upon us; he will subdue our iniquities; and thou wilt cast all their sins into the depths of the sea' (Mic. 7:18,19).

But we must go on to a third observation on the words: 'And when he came to himself, he said, How many hired servants of my father's have bread enough and to spare, and I perish with hunger!' Consider, therefore, *that the prodigal son here reveals a grasp of the need for help outside himself, if he is to be helped at all.* What we have said already leads inevitably to this. That black hopelessness of his which made him to cry, 'I perish with hunger,' is a hopelessness in which at first there seems to be no ray of light, no possibility of any kind of assistance or deliverance. There he is in that far country, without so much as the means even to sustain life. He lacks food and covets the very husks eaten by the

CHAPTER 4

swine. The man could scarcely sink any lower than that. He has turned away from his father, rejected his father's love, repudiated the promises of the covenant of grace to which that father clung with all his heart; he has taken his father's substance and wasted it with riotous living in the far country of his heart's desire. A great distance separates him from what he once had and took for granted and came to despise.

Nor is it only a physical distance. As events were to show, though one is nearly starved to death and in an emaciated condition physically, yet it is possible to go a great distance somehow and to return to the father's house. No, the distance is not merely a physical one, to be measured in terms of miles. If it were only that, the problem would not be nearly so overwhelming. The chief element in that distance is spiritual. He has forfeited what was once his by right. He has claimed his inheritance prematurely. He has thrown it all away. And now he perishes, cut off from human sympathy, cut off from help, because of his own fault, and his own sin, and his own perversity. He has no basis, in his own eyes, for appealing to his father or for aspiring to a recovery of his father's love. That love he had never lost, of course. We know that. Jesus makes that abundantly evident in this great parable on the love of God. But he, the prodigal, had no such knowledge. It did not occur to him that his father would be standing there by the wayside, eagerly longing for the day of his return. So far as he was aware, that love and that relationship which he had enjoyed, the sonship which he deliberately abandoned, were gone forever.

But even so, you see what direction his thoughts are beginning to take. At first when his money was gone he went and joined himself to a citizen of that country; and he sent him into his fields to feed swine. There he was, relying upon his own ability to rescue himself, an ability which utterly failed. Now, however, when he has come to himself, he begins to muse and to think and to say, 'How many hired servants of my father's have bread enough and to spare, and I perish with hunger!' His thoughts thus are beginning to turn toward his father! Mind you, they are not very confident thoughts. 'I will arise,' he said to himself, 'I will arise and go to my father, and will say unto him, Father, I have sinned against heaven, and before thee, and am no more worthy to be called thy son: make me as one of thy hired servants.' His highest aspiration here is to become a servant in his father's household. No more than that! How little he knew that father! How incompletely he understood him! 'Like as a father pitieth his children, so the Lord pitieth them that fear him. For he knoweth our frame; he remembereth that we are dust' (Ps. 103:13,14). The prodigal had no notion of that. This was all strange to him still, and it was only afterward that he came to experience the fatherly compassion and mercy of God.

But as least there is a soundness about his sense of direction. 'How many hired servants of *my father's!*' The name is there, the title is there, and the old relationship so long since abandoned is taking on form again. His awakened, convicted condition points him once more to the only source of help: not in that far country, not in the service of one of its citizens, not in the feeding of swine, not in despair and doubt and hopelessness, but in the father and the father's house! What a great thing it is to have even a faint glimmering, a tiny ray of hope, to begin to recover oneself, or rather: to begin to be recovered, for it was not in the prodigal at all that rescue lay, but in the constant, steadfast, unalterable love of God! And we do not learn the meaning of the parable aright unless we understand that any one of us, in our sin, and failure and lostness, may also turn to think of that home of all homes, of the Father of all fathers, of God and his love for sinners!

> *With broken heart and contrite sigh,*
> *A trembling sinner, Lord, I cry;*
> *Thy pard'ning grace is rich and free:*
> *O God, be merciful to me!*
>
> *I smite upon my troubled breast,*
> *With deep and conscious guilt oppressed,*
> *Christ and his cross my only plea:*
> *O God, be merciful to me!*
>
> *Far off I stand with tearful eyes,*
> *Nor dare uplift them to the skies;*
> *But thou dost all my anguish see:*
> *O God, be merciful to me!*
>
> *(Cornelius Elven)*

5. 'I Will Arise and Go to My Father'

*A*s we have traced the spiritual history of the young man who is at the heart of the story the nature of his sin has become clear to us, and so has the dawning in his mind and heart of a deep sense of need. The best thing that ever happened to the prodigal son was the disappearance of his capital; for it was not until his money was gone that he began to understand the true character of his wretchedness. His reduction to the status of a beggar seeking bread from others taught him the beggarly condition of his soul. And he desperately needed that medicine. 'He began to be in want': that is to say, he came at last, haltingly and painfully but nevertheless surely, to perceive his own want and misery and position of estrangement from his father.

The Lord Jesus Christ also gives us to know the next step in the prodigal's recovery. 'And when he came to himself, he said, How many hired servants of my father's have bread enough and to spare, and I perish with hunger!' How I like those words: 'And when he came to himself!' What volumes they speak! He began to recover soundness of mind.

His understanding returned to him. As we have seen, the expression teaches us that the young man now has a grasp of his true condition. He has come to be under a genuine conviction of sin, and in that conviction he reveals an understanding of his remediless hopelessness left to himself and his own devices. In the far country he begins to think once more of his father and his father's house. 'And when he came to himself, he said, How many hired servants of my father's have bread enough and to spare, and I perish with hunger!' He has begun to show also a grasp of the need for help outside himself if he is to be helped at all. That darkness of his which made him cry 'I perish with hunger' is a black hopelessness in which there seems at first to be no light at all, but the direction his thoughts are beginning to take is of immense significance. Driven now to an end of himself, without any more confidence or expectation that he can effect his own rescue, he turns in his mind back to his father and his home.

You see what signs there are of a recovery in the prodigal's mind. No longer is there any residual desire for what the far country had to offer. With his ability to purchase its pleasures had gone his desire to do so as well. The shackles of bondage to his own sinful inclinations are being struck off his hands and his feet. It is a strange thing, surely, that there should be such great confusion at just this point. In the minds of many people freedom is to be identified with unrestraint, being what one will, doing what one wants whenever one wants, no matter what the circumstances. To throw off bonds and obligations, to be rid of moral and religious precepts which have come down to us from a past we no longer understand and do not care to understand, to have the right of unlimited self-expression in whatever forms we desire: this is supposed to be freedom, and an enviable kind of thing.

But if you stop to think about it—and any one who deals regularly with people is quite aware of this fact—what this really means is a new and much more terrible bondage than the old restraint ever was: a bondage, that is, to one's own wickedness and lust. When a man follows this line of reasoning and identifies freedom with unrestraint and license, with doing as he pleases, he is only binding himself and all those under his influence with the chains of sin from which there is no human hope of deliverance. The Apostle Paul is speaking of this very thing when he writes: 'Know ye not, that to whom ye yield yourselves servants to obey, his servants ye are to whom ye obey: whether of sin unto death, or of obedience unto righteousness?' (Rom. 6:16). There are only two relationships in which one can stand in this respect: one is either a slave to sin or a slave to God. A third alternative does not exist. The prodigal had been the former. O yes, he had been a slave to sin and now knew what that meant from the inside. What he had thought of as freedom was the fearful bondage of that far country, the bondage of sin, the bondage of his own insatiable desires. But now the direction of his life was beginning to change. The ruin of his hopes had at the same time shown him the destitution and poverty of his soul. He was weary of having his own way, tired of doing as he pleased, and completely unfulfilled. 'I perish with hunger!'

Do you wonder then that I said that the best thing that ever happened to this young man was the loss of his money and his possessions? Had he never run through them all and been left penniless and without help in the far country, he would not have come to see that the answer to his problems did not lie in more of the same, and that if he were to be healed and redeemed and restored and fulfilled this must come from outside himself. Indeed, at this stage he already knew what he had to do, where he had to go. We have seen that there is a soundness about the prodigal's sense of direction here which is worthy of remark. He begins to think of his father's house. His understanding is still very limited in terms of what he expects from his father. After all, when wrong has been done and a relationship broken, the guilty one can scarcely expect the one offended to receive him as before. There is certainly no presumptuousness about the prodigal now. 'How many hired servants of my father's have bread enough and to spare!' That is the direction, but also at the same time the limitation of his thinking. The great thing to observe here is that the young man has reached the point at which he is prepared to act upon the soundness of mind which has been restored to him. He has come to himself indeed. The old has begun to pass away.

We are concerned now in what follows to examine more closely the subsequent verses in the parable: 'I will arise and go to my father, and will say unto him, Father, I have sinned against heaven, and before thee, and am no more worthy to be called thy son: make me as one of thy hired servants. And he arose, and came to his father.' These are immensely significant words, for in them there is a description of what we may call evangelical repentance, or repentance unto life. 'What is repentance unto life?' asks the Westminster Shorter Catechism. And then it answers: 'Repentance unto life is a saving grace, whereby a sinner, out of a true sense of his sin, and apprehension of the mercy of God in Christ, doth, with grief and hatred of his sin, turn from it unto God, with full purpose of, and endeavor after,

new obedience' (Q. 87). That is a striking and accurate definition of the extremely important manner which engages us
here.

If we study the biblical teaching on repentance, we shall
discover that repentance is the very threshold of one's experience of the grace of God. It is not the first step in salvation. As we have seen already, many things have gone
before in the prodigal's own life. And to say only that is to
leave unsaid all that the Scriptures reveal to us about God's
great plan of salvation which goes back even beyond the
foundation of the world. Christ whom men took and by
wicked hands crucified and put to death, the Apostle Peter
tells us, was 'delivered by the determinate counsel and
foreknowledge of God' (Acts 2:23). Nevertheless, repentance is the first conscious step in a person's experience of
the divine grace, the entrance for all believers into life,
hope, and salvation.

As we examine this aspect of the parable of the son more
closely, we see that there is here *an honest self-appraisal*. It
is precisely that, surely, which is portrayed for us in the
words: 'I will arise and go to my father, and will say unto
him, Father, I have sinned against heaven and before thee.'

This is by no means an easy thing to do, this assessing of
one's mind and heart and conscience. The process is painful
in the extreme and can be so horrifying that a person may
despair of himself in the course of it. No doubt a distinction
ought to be drawn here between that self-appraisal which
initiates repentance unto life and that shocking, terrifying,
dismaying awareness of what one is which does not lead one
to take refuge in the mercy of God. It is the difference
between the history of the prodigal son, and of many others

like the Apostle Peter and the Apostle Paul, on the one hand, and that of Judas Iscariot on the other who took the thirty pieces of silver he had received in payment for the betrayal of Christ, cast them down before the chief priests, and then went and hanged himself. Who can forget the utter horror with which, in the ultimate self-discovery, Judas cried, 'I have sinned in that I have betrayed the innocent blood' (Matt. 27:4,5). These two—the sorrow of the world, remorse, intense, overwhelming regret at the consequences of one's actions, and a godly sorrow, repentance unto life—are in some respects very like one another, at least superficially. But they are forever separated by their issue, by the fruits which they produce in the end.

In preaching the gospel one is under constant constraint to remind people time and again that there is no need for despair in contemplating one's sins. The mercy of God is limitless, and one ought never to doubt the sufficiency of the sacrifice of Christ to cover all sins, no matter how aggravated, how gross, how serious they may be. At the same time, however, though it may be true that sometimes ministers neglect to keep holding up before people's minds the truth of the infinite goodness and grace of God, there is also another danger lying precisely on the other side: it is the danger of so accentuating and stressing the mercy of God that his justice, his holiness, his righteousness are forgotten. In that case one comes under the condemnation of the Scriptures pronounced against those who 'have healed also the hurt of my people slightly, saying, Peace, peace; when there is no peace' (Jer. 6:14). A degree of tension always exists between these two poles: that of emphasizing the divine mercy and that of underscoring the divine justice; and one is to keep both of them clearly in view.

I suppose that there have been times—certainly there have been specific instances—in which the justice of God was so exclusively thrust into the foreground that people began to think of God as something other than he is revealed to be in his own Word, something much more severe, stern, unbending, merciless, uncompassionate. But I am at pains to point now to the justice and holiness of God because I believe very strongly that the tendency of our own day is quite the opposite. The great emphasis in preaching —and I mean here especially evangelistic preaching—is not upon the need for understanding ourselves as we really are before the infinite justice and holiness of God, but upon inducing an impression or a general feeling of spiritual need, whereupon people without more ado are immediately referred to the practice of what is called 'accepting Christ' or 'letting him into one's heart,' with the idea that all this can be got through in a few minutes of time. But a necessarily instantaneous approach to these things is most certainly not in accord with the pattern and the examples of Scripture. To be sure, one can come to Christ very quickly indeed. But the process can also be much more extended than that. It may take only a short period. But it may also take much longer. Time is not the important thing.

The notion that repentance may be identified with the fleeting awareness of some personal inadequacy, or with regret on account of the consequences of sin, is an error which in the end may do more harm than good. We are naturally disposed to think of repentance as an easy, short-lived, transient thing, and we will not readily accept any teaching which encourages in us a sense of the need for the honest appraisal of self that we find so clearly represented in the life of the prodigal son. I do not mean in any sense at all to deprecate evangelism. On the contrary, I believe firmly that we do not engage in nearly enough activity which is directly evangelistic. As Christians we are far too hesitant to tell men and women that they need to be saved. There are various ways of doing that, and each person is to be treated as an individual. We cannot follow a certain set pattern always on all occasions, without giving the distinct impression that the pattern is more significant than the people whom the message of the gospel is intended to reach. The chief thing, however, is that we be obedient to the Scriptures and do not trim our sails for the sake of some immediate but passing results. It is one thing to tell people that they are sinners and in need of the salvation of God. It is another to make them understand what it means that they are sinners, to make them sense that fact, to make them consciously aware of it with the help, the indispensable help, of the Holy Spirit, so that they are caused to cry out, 'What must I do to be saved?'

The paramount need in this connection is a holy, godly kind of introspection and self-appraisal through which people apprehend the true condition of their lives. If you are not a Christian, if you have no experience of the power of God, if you know yourself to be a sinful man or woman, estranged from God, without hope, without God in the world, then begin honestly and courageously with that fact. Own up to it. Face it. Admit it, to yourself first of all, and to God. You will eventually have to admit it to others as well; but begin with yourself and with God. Look into your heart. See what is really there. Not what you would like to find there, not what fits in with your own image of yourself, not merely what is in harmony with the respectable projection of yourself which you send out into the world, but what is really there. 'Father, I have sinned against heaven, and before thee.'

We must observe further that there is here in this stage of the spiritual pilgrimage of the prodigal son *an open confession of guilt*. This is very apparent indeed in the words, ''I will arise and go to my father, and will say unto him, Father, I have sinned against heaven, and before thee.' The young man is most forthright about it: 'I have sinned,' he says. There is no attempt whatsoever to cover up the fact that he has done wrong, that he has turned his back upon all his privileges as a son in his father's house, and that, estranged from his father, he has wasted his substance in riotous living. The acknowledgement of guilt is altogether clear and quite without any qualification, 'I have sinned.'

What an enormously important thing it is to have reached this stage and to be able to make such a statement! Pictured here is the experience of genuine, searching conviction that John Bunyan so graphically describes in the opening pages of his *Pilgrim's Progress*. You may perhaps remember, if you have read the book (and I hope you have, or will), that he writes:

'As I walked through the wilderness of this world, I lighted on a certain place where was a den, and laid me down in that place to sleep; and, as I slept, I dreamed a dream. I dreamed, and behold I saw a man clothed in rags, standing in a certain place, with his face from his own house, a book in his hand, and a great burden upon his back. I looked, and saw him open the book, and read therein, and as he read he wept and trembled; and not being able longer to contain, he brake out with a lamentable cry, saying, ''What shall I do?''

'In this plight, therefore, he went home, and refrained himself as long as he could, that his wife and children should not perceive his distress; but he could not be silent long, because that his trouble increased; wherefore, at length, he brake his mind to his wife and children, and thus he began to talk to them: "O! my dear wife," said he, "and you the children of my bowels, I, your dear friend, am in myself undone, by reason of a burden that lieth hard upon me: moreover, I am for certain informed, that this our city will be burned with fire from heaven; in which fearful overthrow both myself, with thee my wife, and you my sweet babes, shall miserably come to ruin except (the which yet I see not) some way of escape may be found, whereby we may be delivered." '

His wife and children were, of course, amazed at his behavior and did not know how to take it. Is not this always the case when unconverted persons are confronted with a man in the grip of a conviction of sin and wrestling with God? They regarded his state of mind as a derangement, and sought to shake him loose from it in various ways, none of which was of any avail at all. Instead, his conviction and sense of foreboding grew worse and worse. 'Now,' says Bunyan, continuing his narrative, 'I saw, upon a time, when he was walking in the fields, that he was (as he was wont) reading his book, and greatly distressed in his mind; and, as he read, he burst out as he had done before, crying, "What shall I do to be saved?"

'I saw also, that he looked this way and that way, as if he would run; yet he stood still, because (as I perceived) he could not tell which way to go. I looked then, and saw a man named Evangelist coming to him, and asked, "Wherefore dost thou cry?"

'He answered, "Sir, I perceive, by the book in my hand, that I am condemned to die, and after that to come to judgment; and I find that I am not willing to do the first, nor able to do the second."

'Then said Evangelist, "Why not willing to die, since this life is attended with so many evils?" The man answered, "Because I fear that this burden that is upon my back [that is, the burden of sin] will sink me lower than the grave, and I shall fall into Tophet. And, Sir, if I be not fit to go to prison, I am not fit to go to judgment, and from thence to execution; and the thoughts of these things make me cry."

'Then said Evangelist, "If this be thy condition, why standest thou still?" He answered, "Because I know not whither to go." Then he gave him a parchment roll, and there was written within, "Fly from the wrath to come" ' (Matt. 3:7).

It is just the same quality which characterizes the present condition of the prodigal son, this restless, ceaseless unease in sin and in separation from God, this conviction of wrong-doing and of guilt. It issues forth from the honest self-appraisal of which we have spoken. When a man begins to examine his own heart, under the influence of the Holy Spirit and with the application of the law of God, that soul-illuminating law before which no flesh can stand, he comes to see that he is a sinner; and he is struck down by the horror of what he is and what he has done. You see, our conduct is never a private matter. Even our innermost thoughts and desires which appear to have no other reference than to our own secret lives, which seem to bear no relationship to other people and which cannot be said to harm or damage our fellowmen, even these are not impersonal matters for which we bear no responsibility or guilt and which fall under the category of 'our own business.' Such is our responsibility before God that nothing is impersonal. All the aspects and facets of our lives have a God-ward direction, a reference to the One who created us and before whom we stand for judgment.

This is a lesson we must all learn, and learn before it is too late for any remedy. And yet how hard it is for us to do so! How readily and frequently we fend off the accusations of conscience and the Word of God with a reference to the general human condition. I have heard people do this again and again. But a true confession of guilt, the kind of confession that shows the process of a true conviction and repentance within us, demands that we have done with such excuses. Other people are unimportant for the moment here. It will not help you in the end that others are sinful, too, and that you are not alone in having broken the law of God. To be sure, 'all have sinned, and come short of the glory of God' (Rom. 3:23); but that 'all' does not take away the necessity for remembering very specifically, and understanding beyond all question and doubt, that it is you personally who are involved. You have sinned. You have come short of the divine glory. You are under the just sentence of death. You must appear before the judgment seat of Christ. And if your sins are to be cleared away, you must flee from the wrath to come. You must openly and unqualifiedly confess your sins to God, just as the prodigal did, and just as Bunyan's pilgrim did. 'Father, I have sinned against heaven and before thee.' There are no conditions here, no reticences, no attempts at self-justification. 'I have sinned.'

> *Before thee, God, who knowest all,*
> *With grief and shame I prostrate fall.*
> *I see my sins against thee, Lord,*

The sins of thought, of deed, and word.
They press me sore; I cry to thee:
O God be merciful to me!

O Lord, my God, to thee I pray:
O cast me not in wrath away!
Let thy good Spirit ne'er depart,
But let him draw to thee my heart,
That truly penitent I be:
O God, be merciful to me!

(Magnus B. Landstad, tr. by Carl Döving)

We cannot leave the prodigal at this stage of his life before noting that besides confession of guilt there is in him also *a genuine turning from sin and an anxious turning to God.* Repentance—the repentance of which the Scriptures speak as a godly sorrow, the repentance which is unto life— is not only a persuasion of sinfulness, but it is also, and very distinctly, a turning from sin. Remember those words of the Westminster Confession of Faith, here as always so very faithful to the teaching of the Word of God itself: By repentance 'a sinner, out of the sight and sense, not only of the danger, but also of the filthiness and odiousness of his sins, as contrary to the holy nature and righteous law of God, and upon the apprehension of his mercy in Christ to such as are penitent, so grieves for and hates his sins, as to turn from them all unto God, purposing and endeavoring to walk with him in all ways of his commandments' (XV/1).

One must be very clear on this point, particularly in view of the fact that it is not always understood by all those who call themselves Christians. In discussions of Christian teaching a distinction has sometimes been drawn, for example, between 'contrition' and 'attrition.' Contrition is the true evangelical repentance which we have been at pains to define. Attrition, on the other hand, is something very different. Though it has been held by some to be a valid form of repentance, yet it is far from what the Scriptures demand. Sorrow for sin may have many motives. Attrition, in the theological sense of the word, is a kind of repentance which results from fear of punishment. That is to say, attrition is the conviction that sin deserves to be judged, but it does not involve trust in God and the steadfast purpose to turn away from disobedience to him. It is based on the fear of hell, and is the acknowledgement of God's wrath upon and determination to punish sin, not the indispensable turning away from sin, 'purposing and endeavoring to walk with God in all the ways of his commandments.'

People may come to regret a life of sin and of disobedience to God for a variety of reasons: they may have been found out in it; they may have discovered sin's fruitlessness and frustrating, empty, unsatisfying character; they may even have come to fear the divine judgment seat before which we all must stand at last. But unless they have by the grace of God turned their backs upon sin, theirs is not the repentance which marks the life of the prodigal son at this point and which must mark every man who comes to God.

This is an area in which the Scriptures admit of no misunderstanding whatsoever. 'Repent, and turn yourselves from all your transgressions; so iniquity shall not be your ruin. Cast away from you all your transgressions, whereby ye have transgressed; and make you a new heart and a new spirit: for why will ye die, O house of Israel?' (Ezek. 18:30,31). 'For godly sorrow worketh repentance to salvation not to be repented of: but the sorrow of the world worketh death' (2 Cor. 7:10). Christ made Paul a minister to the Gentiles, the Lord himself told the apostle, 'to open their eyes, and to turn them from darkness to light, and from the power of Satan unto God, that they may receive forgiveness of sins, and inheritance among them which are sanctified by faith that is in me' (Acts 26:18). These references could, of course, be supplemented with many others. Everywhere the Word of God reminds us that repentance is not simply honesty with oneself, or even the open confession of one's sins; it must also lead to a *forsaking* of them. If it does not do that, if it is only the fear of punishment and of hell, only a trembling before the just judgment of God, without at the same time the purposing to turn away from sin and to undertake a new obedience to God, then it is not repentance at all.

I have already made reference to those striking pages at the opening of John Bunyan's *Pilgrim's Progress*, in which the pilgrim is warned by Evangelist 'to flee from the wrath to come' (Matt. 3:7): After reading this solemn message, 'and, looking upon Evangelist very carefully, [he] said, "Whither must I fly?" Then said Evangelist, pointing with his finger over a very wide field, "Do you see yonder wicket-gate?" The man said, "No." Then said the other, "Do you see yonder shining light?" He said, "I think I do." Then said Evangelist, "Keep that light in your eye, and go up directly thereto, so shalt thou see the gate; at which, when thou knockest, it shall be told thee what thou shalt do."

'So I saw in my dream,' Bunyan continues, 'that the man began to run: now, he had not run far from his own door, but his wife and children, perceiving it, began to cry after him to return; but the man put his fingers in his ears, and ran on, crying, "Life! Life! Eternal Life!" So he looked not behind him, but fled towards the middle of the plain.

'The neighbours also came out to see him run, and as he ran, some mocked, others threatened and some cried after him to return; and among those that did so, there were two that resolved to fetch him back by force; the name of the one was Obstinate, and name of the other Pliable. Now, by this time, the man was got a good distance from them; but however, they were resolved to pursue him, which they did, and in a little time they overtook him. Then said the man, "Neighbours, wherefore are ye come?" They said, "To persuade you to go back with us;" but he said, "That can by no means be. You dwell," said he, "in the City of Destruction (the place also where I was born); I see it to be so; and dying there, sooner or later, you will sink lower than the grave, into a place that burns with fire and brimstone. Be content, good neighbours, and go along with me."

' "What!" said Obstinate, "and leave our friends and our comforts behind us.?"

' "Yes," said Christian (for that was his name), "because that all which you forsake is not to be compared with a little of that that I am seeking to enjoy; and if you will go along with me, and hold it, you shall fare as I myself; for there, where I go, is enough and to spare. Come away, and prove my words."

' "What," asked Obstinate, "are the things you seek, since you leave all the world to find them?"

' "I seek," said Christian, "an inheritance incorruptible, undefiled, and that fadeth not away; and it is laid up in heaven and safe there, to be bestowed, at the time appointed, on them that diligently seek it. Read it so, if you will, in my book." '

The lesson here is surely sufficiently plain. Take particular note of the sequence in the passage we have before us (Luke

15:18,19,20a). The prodigal son says, 'I will arise and go to my father, and will say unto him, Father, I have sinned against heaven, and before thee.' And then follow the words, 'And he arose, and came to his father.' He put the far country behind his back. He had done with the sinning, and the grieving, and the wretchedness and the despair of that land of his near-ruin and personal disaster. He did not content himself with bemoaning his condition, and bewailing the privileges he had lost. He turned his back upon it, he left it, he came away. That, you see, is a fundamental part of the true, evangelical repentance of which the Scriptures speak.

There are many people who talk a great deal about the sorrow and grief they experience because of sin. One sees this time and again in connection with evangelistic preaching. They respond to the offer of the gospel. They make a profession of faith in the Lord Jesus Christ. They look into their own hearts, and they confess and acknowledge their sins, sometimes at considerable length. But when the impression has faded, and the emotional drive has disappeared, they soon fall back again into the same life of sin and of godlessness which they led before. They prove by their subsequent actions that all their '*talk*' of repentance was only that: it was mere 'talk,' and nothing more. There is no genuine repentance without turning from sin.

It is significant that the Greek word for 'repentance' employed in the New Testament *(metanoia)* quite specifically includes the idea of which we are now speaking. It means 'a change of mind,' 'conversion,' 'a reversal in the direction of one's life,' an 'about-face.' In the nature of the case, therefore, to repent is not only to do something of a negative character, that is, to put sin away; it is also highly positive, that is, it involves turning away from disobedience and sin and looking instead toward God.

You will notice how very evident this aspect of repentance is in the history of the prodigal son. We have had cause time and again to recollect that for a long time he set his face away from his father. His sorrows began when he demanded his inheritance of his father. He wanted what would come to him afterward for the reason that he was so eager to have done with the restrictions and confinement of his father's house. And when he had secured what he desired, we are told, 'not many days after the younger son gathered all together, and took his journey into a far country, and there wasted his substance with riotous living.' During all that time he did as much as to blot out of his memory his father's face and his father's name. When his money was spent, and he had nothing, even then he did not turn about and go back to the home he had left. No indeed! Rather, he sought instead to fill his belly with the husks that the swine did eat. He tried his own remedies and his own devices. He thought to help himself. It was only when he came to himself, and had at last a dawning consciousness of the magnitude of his offense, only when he began to understand the devastating extent of his condition of alienation and separation from his father, that other thoughts sprang up within him, by the grace of God, and the father-ward, home-ward, God-ward journey began as well. Now, rather than to look backward and toward sin and disobedience and rebellion, he looks forward and toward his father and forgiveness and reconciliation.

> *Take me, O my Father, take me;*
> *Take me, save me, through thy Son;*
> *That which thou wouldst have me, make me,*

Let thy will in me be done.
Long from thee my footsteps straying,
Thorny proved the way I trod;
Weary come I now, and praying,
Take me to thy love, my God.

Fruitless years with grief recalling,
Humbly I confess my sin;
At thy feet, O Father, falling,
To thy household take me in.
Freely now to thee I proffer
This relenting heart of mine;
Freely life and soul I offer,
Gift unworthy love like thine.

Once the world's Redeemer, dying,
Bore our sins upon the tree;
On that sacrifice relying,
Now I look in hope to thee;
Father, take me; all forgiving,
Fold me to thy loving breast;
In thy love for ever living
I must be for ever blest.

(Ray Palmer)

This has always been the experience of those who have come to God. It is perhaps nowhere more strikingly illustrated than in the lives of notable men who entered the Christian ministry in an unconverted state and who had to learn with much pain and anguish the need to turn from themselves and their own sin to the mercy of God in the Lord Jesus Christ. One thinks here of Martin Luther, the great Reformer who for years sought peace for a troubled conscience in all the devices and remedies of the church but who found it only when he abandoned himself in faith to God. Or Alexander Henderson, afterwards the leader of the

Second Reformation in Scotland, who came under conviction of sin and learned to look to Christ through the preaching of Robert Bruce. Or John Wesley, the mighty evangelist of the Methodist revival in the eighteenth century, who first groped for life in the hopeless striving for a righteousness of his own but at last discovered the joy of God through forsaking himself and lifting his heart to the Saviour.

Few men exemplify a turning from sin to God more beautifully and more powerfully than Abraham Kuyper, one of the towering Christian theologians and political leaders of the last hundred years. Kuyper had a vast influence especially in his own country, the Netherlands, but also in the United States and in other parts of the world. He was a forceful preacher of the gospel, the founder of a great university, the head of an important Christian political party, a theologian with few equals, and for some years prime minister of his country. His *Stone Lectures on Calvinism* given at Princeton Theological Seminary in 1898 remain a classic on the subject. But Abraham Kuyper entered the ministry with no saving knowledge of Christ or of repentance. It was in the early years of his ministry in a country parish that he came into contact with a group of narrow, uneducated, uncultivated people who were also earnest Christians with a high view of God and a keen insight into the meaning of salvation. Kuyper had a brilliant mind and had received a superb education. He was a man of culture and refinement, earnest, religious, zealous for truth, moral, respectable, but at the same time a prodigal son estranged from the Father.

It was through his acquaintance with these plain Christian people that Dr. Kuyper came to see his own need and the only way to its fulfilment. One young woman in particular, Pietronella Baltus, was wonderfully used in his life.

When he came to visit in her home she began to deal with him about the character of his sermons and to urge on him the necessity of *his* conversion, of his taking refuge in the blood of Christ. One might have expected a haughty disdain on the part of a man like Kuyper for what seemed to be an act of religious impertinence, but instead he was deeply impressed, and out of the hunger of his own heart returned often to speak with her. And in the end Kuyper broke with the helpless liberalism that had held his mind in its sway, abandoned himself, and turned in faith to the only Saviour of sinners. All his life he remained grateful for the goodness of God which had led him to Pietronella Baltus and others like her. And almost half a century later, when she died in 1914 at the age of eighty-four, Dr. Kuyper who had reached the pinnacle of his fame at home and abroad was not ashamed, as editor of one of the leading newspapers of the country, in commenting on her death to tell the world that it was this woman who had shown him himself and led him to turn his face to the Lord Jesus Christ.

These experiences of Luther and Henderson and Wesley and Kuyper could be multiplied many times, of course, and they have their parallels in the lives of thousands and millions of believers throughout history, perhaps in your life, too. They are but illustrations of what the Lord is teaching us in this parable of the prodigal son when he shows the young man to be turning at last from his sin and from the world and from his lostness and from his estrangement, to his father and his father's house.

But there is something else that must be added here. I said earlier that there is in these verses an *anxious* turning to God. There is nothing boastful or presumptuous about the prodigal. You notice that in his own words: 'I am no more worthy to be called thy son: make me as one of thy hired servants.' He does not take his father for granted. He does not assume any kind of full restoration to sonship. He only knows that he is lost as he is, and without hope, and that his only alternative, the only thing that holds out any remedy at all, is that long-since-forsaken home and his father's compassion and love. He sees that he has forfeited his rights as a son, and determines only to plead for a servant's place and a servant's life within the shelter of that dear, homely, loving house. That is all. It is just so that we must come. It is to God through Christ we are to come, but pleading nothing, no right, no privilege, no prerogative, no righteousness of our own—only the divine mercy.

> *Nothing in my hand I bring,*
> *Simply to thy cross I cling;*
> *Naked, come to thee for dress,*
> *Helpless, look to thee for grace;*
> *Foul, I to the fountain fly;*
> *Wash me, Saviour, or I die.*

(A. M. Toplady)

6. 'Father!'

We have come a long way in our study of Jesus' parable of the prodigal son. But we have a distance to travel still, and the best is yet to be. Just as it is important to know that the end of life, the end of sinful human life, need not be in a far country, so it is also important to understand that repentance is not an end in itself, that it points toward something, or rather, toward Someone, and that what really matters at last is not the sinner's frame of mind and heart, but the receiving mercy of God.

Thus far we have observed the prodigal in his far country resolving to arise and go to his father. A sound mind has been restored to him. He now knows again what he is about. He is convinced that there is no help for him estranged from his home. And he determines to say to his father, 'Father, I have sinned against heaven, and before thee, and am no more worthy to be called thy son; make me as one of thy hired servants.' We are told, moreover, that he in fact 'arose, and came to his father.'

But therein lies the crux of the matter. What if the prodigal, resolved upon humbling himself before his father, had been rejected, and spurned, and cast aside? He deserved that, no doubt. His lack of natural affection, his wastrel's life, his wilful and wicked withdrawal from all that was good and true and holy, had brought disaster upon him, and there was no one to blame but himself. Nevertheless, what a sad state of affairs it would be were that all, and if nothing more could be said than that sin is forever sin, and that the consequences of sin are forever irremovable.

What if that father were not there? What if, after so many years of alienation and separation and disappointment and grief, the father had hardened his heart, and turned aside from waiting, and given up hope of ever seeing or receiving his son again? What if the father had decided to treat the prodigal in precisely the manner which his misconduct and sin deserved? What if, upon the completion of the long, wearisome journey from the far country to his homeland, after all those days and hours and minutes of anticipation and resolve, the young man saw no father to greet him, no father before whom to kneel down, no father from whom to supplicate favor, no father to forgive him and to restore him at least to a servant's place in his household? What if? What if? What if? You see how these questions multiply themselves, and rebound upon each other. What is a prodigal son without a waiting father? Is there any comfort in the story of a sinner, if that sinner does not come home, finds no reception, is not healed, restored, and forgiven?

There could not possibly be any more important question than that which is involved here. Interpersonal relationships are, of course, tremendously significant. How we treat one another, how we view our responsibilities toward one another, how we are to be just and honourable and caring and compassionate over against our fellowmen—these considerations are not to be downgraded or made anything less than vital to us all. But the grave error of the present time is that men have somehow come to think of such matters as the sum and substance of the moral and spiritual part of life, have fallen prey to the notion that correcting our common inhumanity to one another is all that really counts in the end. The vast and critical dimension of the father and the father's house has been lost to view. We are no longer concerned about the issue of sin in terms of its God-ward direction, no longer interested in the absolutely basic vertical relationship of man to God without which nothing else has any meaning, and in the absence of an awareness of which even right human relationships lack foundation and support.

I say again that there could not possibly be a more important question than that which is before us now. You have perhaps never stopped to ask yourself any questions having to do with life and death. You have deliberately ignored the issues of sin and of grace, thinking that if you kept to yourself as much as possible, refrained from doing any serious damage to others, lived as much as you could by the golden rule, all would be well in the end. Further than that you have not wished to go. Religion is a harmless pastime for people who are inclined toward that sort of thing, and a bow in the direction of God at public ceremonies—the opening of a court session, a commencement exercise, some patriotic celebration—is probably a good thing. But to take the Bible seriously, to admit that you are a sinner and in need of a Saviour, of a waiting Father, of God and his Son Jesus Christ: that is quite another matter.

If it is any comfort to you, in these thoughts and ideas

you are by no means alone. There are many besides you who reason along these lines, or, at least, who live as though they reason along these lines, though it is usually not so much a process of thought as it is of simply taking life as it comes and ignoring ultimate issues. Indeed, there are also church members enough and to spare who think, or at any rate act, on these same lines. One of the disturbing things about the church today is that while our rolls are swollen with the names of people who would not contemplate any other state of affairs than that they should be registered as Presbyterians or Episcopalians or Baptists or Methodists or whatever, and who would be grievously offended, not to say shocked, were anyone to suggest removing them, yet those membership rolls are but sadly represented in the actual life of the church. And when it comes to an active personal Christian life, a life of interest in the things of God, and when it comes to displaying what the Apostle Paul calls the 'mind of the Spirit,' there is often little evidence of Christian fruitfulness, of repentance and conversion and the obedience of faith.

The Word of God makes it clear that one of the duties of the church is the administration of discipline, and that those who take no part in the life of the congregation to which they profess to belong, who apparently care nothing about the gospel, who never give any indication of a saving relationship with the Lord Jesus Christ, have no place in the church, and should be dealt with in such a way as to remind them plainly and lovingly that they, just as others who have no connection with the church, need to turn to God and to seek his face. No indeed, you who are indifferent are not alone. And that is not surprising. We are told in the Bible that 'the whole world lieth in wickedness' (1 John 5:19), a wickedness just as great and just as aggravated and just as serious and just as much in need of being repented of as the wickedness of the prodigal son.

It is a distressing thing that there should be such a widespread failure to understand this profound truth, such a tendency to insist upon rather less than do the Scriptures in the preaching of the gospel. There are those who want to rub off the rough edges of truth, and to make the way to God less demanding, less arduous, less humbling to the sinner than the Lord has ordained it to be. A general acknowledgement of need, a momentary consciousness of personal inadequacy, a vague profession of faith linked with a sentimental notion of Christ, a loose, undemanding relationship to the church and the life of faith—these are the only qualifications they require for membership in the church and the right of men and women to call themselves Christians. I fear that large numbers of people—perhaps you among them— are deceiving themselves into thinking that because they are permitted to stay registered upon the rolls of a church, and because they persist in giving lip service to a belief in the Scriptures and the Christ they present, all is well with them, and nothing more can be required. But, my friend, it is not so. God does not stand behind and guarantee the pledge of every careless minister and every lax congregation. And not a jot or a tittle has been removed from the unqualified, stark, utterly humbling demand of repentance and faith.

But the fact that you are in a large company, surrounded by great numbers of like-minded people, has no real significance. When did mere numbers become the criterion for determining the truth? It does not count in your favor that you are going to hell with a host of companions. And the gross spiritual darkness and indifference of the present time only make it more urgent for the gospel to be preached in clarity and power, and for me to tell you as best I know how that we are dealing with the most important and most fundamental issue a man or a woman can possibly face: the issue of your relationship to God. My friend, you need to be saved. You need God. You need him because of your sins and because those sins have hid his face from you. You need him because he created you for his glory and because you are lost without him. You need him because apart from him life has no real meaning. You need him because unless you find him you will go to hell.

People intensely dislike the sound of that word—hell! It has become unpopular to use it, I suppose, largely because so many have ceased to believe in it, though the Scriptures themselves are clear enough on that point. I am not employing the word as a threat, not seeking to make a whip of it in order somehow to drive you along forcibly in the direction of faith and of God. That would do no good. I am simply telling you a fact: that without God, without God in Christ, without the waiting father of the parable of the prodigal son, you will most certainly go to hell. Now with that prospect before you, you must surely see the truth of what I have said: that the issues which engage us here are absolutely important and fundamental. You need him. O how you need him! You cannot *live* without him.

Man's spiritual loneliness without God is surely the final lesson impressed upon us by the prodigal son on the eve of his return to his home. The friends whose company had satisfied him at the first are no more with him. They had stood by him, and shared in his life, so long as the money lasted. But when it was gone, they were gone, too. Fair weather friends they were; friends who would sell themselves and their integrity for a little pleasure, but who had no interest whatsoever in helping someone in need, and in sharing the burden and cares of a poor beggar. And so, penniless, self-impoverished, destitute, forced to take refuge in the meanest of employments as a swineherd in a strange land, the prodigal was left alone. He was by himself. There was no one else, none to whom he could turn, none from whom he could even ask charity with any hope of being heard. It seemed as though he were utterly forsaken.

It is a terrible thing, as you may know, to be alone. And there is a great deal more loneliness in this world than we are perhaps often aware of. One thinks of those whom the death of others has left behind; of some whose contemporaries have all passed away and who therefore have no real friends any longer; of others whom life appears to have passed by, who have no husband or wife, or who have been widowed and thus cut off from human companionship and caring. In all our communities, if we only look for them, there are people who feel themselves deserted, unloved, who have no one to love them, to look after them, with whom to share the worries and anxieties and also the joys of life. But physical aloneness is not always or by any means necessarily the worst form of loneliness. Some individuals can live alone, and yet be content. Mitigating factors enter into the picture. Some need less companionship than others. Some indeed, though alone, find that loneliness compensated for by their relationship to God and their daily walk with Christ. A man or a woman can be lonely though surrounded by others and living amid a veritable beehive of activity. I myself can think of few worse experiences of my own than occasions when I was by myself in a strange city where I knew no one and in which there was not a single person to whom I could turn simply to talk. Our great cities are full of lonely people who are constantly crying out in their own, perhaps silent way for something, for someone, and yet whom there is none to help. Yes indeed, the mere physical proximity of other people, even other people in large numbers, means nothing at all in terms of filling the gnawing, aching emptiness of the human spirit which was not meant to dwell alone.

But these brief references to loneliness say nothing at all about the kind of thing the prodigal experienced. He was deserted by his erstwhile friends; so much we have already seen. But I doubt very much that they ever meant anything significant to him even when he had plenty of money and could buy their favor and attentiveness. His relationship to them was a purely external one. They did things together. They enjoyed themselves together. They spent money together. They bought pleasure together. But further than that it could not reach. And the loneliness which the prodigal came to experience afterward was only the outworking of what had been within him all the while, but which he had stamped down and trampled upon, and the existence of which his peace of mind had forced him to deny, until the day came when he began to be in want. Then, then, at long last, he was engulfed and overcome and nearly drowned in wave after wave of the realization of his true position.

Now, mark well: that loneliness of his was not physical in origin. It was not caused by an absence of companionship. But it was brought to light, impressed upon him, by his forsakenness of others. His money spent, his friends gone, his plight desperate, he grew conscious—utterly, starkly conscious—of the condition to which he had sunk. He was alone, far from his father's house. And the only thing that mattered in the end, the only thing that had any meaning in the final analysis, *that* he had spurned, and despised, and rejected. The support, the guiding star by which his life had hitherto been directed, the relationship which was constitutive and decisive for his whole being—his father's love!—that seemed forfeited and gone for ever.

No wonder then that near-despair threatened him, and that his soul was overwhelmed with hopelessness. I say 'near-despair' because the parable takes us beyond that, and shows us something more. But for a time that despair must have seemed total, and his prospects completely dark. Nevertheless, a light begins to dawn upon the gloom and misery of his soul. And herein the prodigal is a mirror and also a pattern to other prodigals: to you, and to me. For any man who comes to God must know first how great his sins and miseries are. And it is only in the dreary blackness of the soul, when we are constrained to come and stand squarely before our failure, our spiritual *aloneness,* our need and our guilt and our blameworthiness and our deservingness of judgment before God and the utter uselessness of our lives without him, that we are in the way of beginning at last to see the breaking of new daylight upon us. You see, the Lord Jesus is teaching us here that after all the prodigal was not altogether alone; and that therefore no man, no woman, so apparently deserted, so given up to near-despair in conviction of sin, is altogether alone either.

There is something here beyond the ken of the forlorn son in the first stages of his spiritual recovery, something which did not appear to him at once, but something of which we know now, and of which he came to know. And what is it but the seeking, saving, all-present love of God for his prodigal sons and daughters, for those in whose stead

Christ came to suffer and to die? The Lord tells us that even despair may lead to light, and that it will most certainly do so if the sinner follows the course of the prodigal son. A statement in the Old Testament Prophecy of Hosea (2:15) puts this very beautifully. Speaking of his people, the Lord said, 'I will give her . . . the valley of Achor for a door of hope.' Achor was the place of the judgment of Achan (Josh. 7) who had stolen treasures from the ruin of Jericho when the children of Israel began to take the Promised Land; it was a symbol of disgrace, of sin, of disobedience, of judgment, of hopelessness. But God declares: I will take that place of wrath and wretchedness in which hope itself has died out, and I will make it instead a very door of hope, a door of restoration and pardon and forgiveness and love.

God can do that, you know. God delights to do that. And the reason is marvellously declared by Christ in words which we shall shortly consider. In brief, we are lost without God and without his redeeming love. There is no final comfort in ourselves or in one another. But our 'What if's,' our doubts, our hesitations, our questions must be answered with the glorious affirmation that *God is,* and that he is love. His love is there, where you are, in your sin, your disobedience, in the ruin you have made of your life, in the seeming dead-endedness and futility of your existence: God's love is there. You are not alone, not really alone, not alone at all. And that love is a guiding, directing, healing, restoring, receiving love for you, just as it was for the prodigal.

> *I waited for the Lord my God,*
> *And patiently did bear;*
> *At length to me he did incline*
> *My voice and cry to hear.*

He took me from a fearful pit,
And from the miry clay,
And on a rock he set my feet,
Establishing my way.

He put a new song in my mouth,
Our God to magnify:
Many shall see it, and shall fear,
And on the Lord rely.

(Psalm 40)

7. 'His Father Saw Him, and had Compassion'

*I*n our study of the parable of the prodigal son we have reached the very heart of what the Lord Jesus Christ is seeking to teach us. We have come, that is, to the meeting of the prodigal with his father, and it is this to which everything has been building up in the details of the story which have gone before. The prodigal himself has, of course, been at mid-stage; but there is Someone behind, beyond, and above him—infinitely above him—Someone transcendently more important than he. And that One is the Father.

You remember that Jesus, while his executioners were in the very act of nailing his bruised body to the cross, prayed aloud those marvellous and forever unforgettable words: 'Father, forgive them, for they know not what they do' (Luke 23:34). His petition was not restricted to the Roman soldiers who had been commanded to put him to death. In a very real sense they were our representatives; they stood in our place; and it was we who drove those spikes through the flesh of the Son of God, we who crucified the Lord of glory. Our sins made his incarnation necessary; he was the Lamb of

God, come to bear away in his own body on the cross the sin of the world. Hence, when he prayed for his executioners, he prayed for us, sinners all, and for every prodigal son and daughter whom he would save.

How fully his Father, the Father of all penitent prodigals, has answered that intercession of his, a thousand thousand examples could be cited to illustrate, from the Scriptures themselves and from the pages of the history of God's people. But there is perhaps no more moving reference to the divine forgiveness, apart from the passion narratives in the gospels, no more affecting and beautiful picture of the love of God, than in the passage we have before us now. 'And he arose, and came to his father. But when he was yet a great way off, his father saw him, and had compassion, and ran, and fell on his neck, and kissed him.'

As we examine these expressions more closely, it becomes clear to us in the first place that *God's love is encompassing and embracing*. It is deep, and it is wide. Remember who this was that the father saw. It was the prodigal son! The immediate proximity of the words 'saw' and 'had compassion' are intended to focus attention upon this fact. 'His father *saw* him, and had compassion.' I do not mean to suggest that the sight of the son's pitiable condition caused compassion to spring up in the father's heart, as though it were not there before. No such idea as that can be gathered from the parable.

What is in view, rather, is the truth that the miserable condition of the sinner is no hindrance to divine love. The prodigal had cut himself off from the sustaining love and care of the father's house, and wasted his father's substance with riotous living. It was he, not the father, who had broken the relationship. It was he who had plunged himself into a life of sin, had degraded himself, had done everything he could to dishonour his own name and that of his father. What a striking contrast there is between him now and as he first appeared at the beginning of the story! We know what has happened to him in the meantime in the far country when the money had gone and he was left destitute and alone, ruined and in very danger of starvation. 'He would fain have filled his belly with the husks that the swine did eat; and no man gave unto him.'

Yes, it was a different person upon whom the father's vision fell when the boy came home again. He was different in appearance. His health was broken. His shoeless feet were marked with open sores, and his emaciated body barely covered with the rags that were all he had left of the finery with which he had set out. But that changed appearance was not the chief thing. For the wretchedness of his physical condition, his ill-health and destitution, now gave accurate reflection of what he had been all along: a sinner, a rebellious, wayward, unappreciative, undeserving, prodigal son. He was good to look upon at first, well-clothed, well-fed, handsome, sure of himself. But he had a heart of wickedness and sin against God. And now the fruit of that evil plant in him, that old nature of his, was clearly to be seen, and could no longer be hidden from any eye, certainly not from the eye of his father.

'His father saw him' in all his sin, his wretchedness, and lostness, 'and had compassion.' The lesson is that the salvation which the gospel brings is a great salvation because it is able to embrace even the worst. The love which comes to those who know their ruin and present themselves before the Father in penitence, seeking forgiveness and restoration, has nothing to do with our deserving. It is entirely a matter of grace. We have forfeited all claim upon the goodness of God; our sin and our rebellion and our rottenness have extended to every part of our being; and if we are to be rescued, if our sins are to be forgiven, if we are to have the hope of eternal life and the resurrection of the dead, then all that must come from him, not from us.

That this understanding of the love of God does not come to us naturally is illustrated by another contrast which Jesus draws here, the contrast between the expectation of the young man and the reception he finds at the hands of the father who runs, and falls on his neck, and embraces him! You will remember that time of mulling these things over in his mind while he was still a swineherd in the far country and wondering what to do, how to approach his father, how to give voice to his sorrow and penitence. 'And when he came to himself, he said, How many hired servants of my father's have bread enough and to spare, and I perish with hunger! I will arise and go to my father, and will say unto him, Father, I have sinned against heaven, and before thee, and am no more worthy to be called thy son: make me as one of thy hired servants.'

One perceives a degree of anxiety and uncertainty in him here. And no wonder! He had, in his own view, no right at all to go back home and present himself as a son to his father. He had once been a son, but he had repudiated that sonship by his insolent behavior and subsequent manner of life. He remained a son, of course; we know that now, from Jesus' words. But the prodigal had no such conviction when he considered the enormity of his misconduct, and the extent of the separation which he, and he alone, had permitted to come between them. O, some glimmering was present, certainly, some dim ray of anticipation and hope. He continued to speak of 'my father.' The family relationship still existed. He was his father's son. He owed his existence to his father, and all he had. But the right and the privilege and the prerogative were gone. And, having begun to be in want, and at length having come to himself, he determines to do the only thing which it appears to him can be done. 'And he arose, and came to his father.'

The only answer to his problems, his only hope, is in his father; and what he had decided to ask is not a son's, but a servant's place in the household he had once so proudly put behind him when he went out to seek his way in the great world. He has something now of the Psalmist's heart who wrote: 'For a day in thy courts is better than a thousand. I had rather be a doorkeeper in the house of my God, than to dwell in the tents of wickedness' (Ps. 84:10). Just to live in that longed for, once deserted, now so blessed father's house, to be a servant there, a doorkeeper, seemed better to him than the comforts and fleshpots and fascinations and soul-destroying corruptness of the far country. He set his mind upon that, and nothing more.

But coming as he did, stripped of all self-righteousness and pleading only the mercy of his father, the prodigal found no servant's place, no doorkeeper's place waiting for him! There is a severe passage in the Old Testament Scriptures giving a stipulation as to the manner in which parents were entitled to deal with a wayward son: 'If a man have a stubborn and rebellious son, which will not obey the voice of his father, or the voice of his mother, and that, when they have chastened him, will not hearken unto them: then shall his father and his mother lay hold on him, and bring him out unto the elders of the city, and unto the gate of his place; and they shall say unto the elders of his city, This our son is stubborn and rebellious, he will not obey our voice; he is a glutton and a drunkard. And all the men of his city shall stone him with stones, that he die: so shalt thou put evil away from among you; and all Israel shall hear, and fear' (Deut. 21:18ff.). That is how the father *could* have treated his son, in the time of his recalcitrance and disobedience and waywardness. But instead we find him waiting. O, those years of waiting! How long they must have seemed and, to a human father, how without prospect, how dark, how hopeless in terms of the prodigal's return! And we find him searching. Did he stand daily by the wayside, squinting his eyes to see farther into the distance in order to know at the first possible instant that the boy was coming home again? Or was he perhaps first apprised of his son's return by one of those hired servants, a place amongst whom the prodigal had come to covet? But above all, we find him loving. His own hurt, the offense against him and his goodness, the degradation, the dishonour of that son's life, all these things, while he did not and could not ignore them, in no respect cancelled out the love he felt for his prodigal son.

What a lesson there is here on the character of God's love! It is the so practical and so necessary truth of which Jesus spoke when he said, 'The Son of man is come to seek and to save that which was lost' (Luke 19:10). And again, 'They that are whole need not a physician; but they that are sick' (Luke 5:31). The compassion of God is not for the proud and the haughty, for those who think themselves whole, for those who suppose they can help themselves, even in remedying the vicious, cancerous condition eating away the vital parts within. 'Who is a God like unto thee, that pardoneth iniquity, and passeth by the transgression of the remnant of his heritage? He retaineth not his anger for ever, because he delighteth in mercy' (Mic. 7:18). The compassion of God is for sinners who come, as this prodigal, seeking grace. 'His father saw him, and had compassion.'

We must observe further as we think of this part of the parable of the prodigal son that God's love is a love with *vast and deep roots*. The Scriptures tell us that the love of God is eternal, and while nothing is said in so many words about this prior character of God's love for sinners in the parable of the prodigal son itself, yet the thought is certainly very evident. What is the one constant factor in the whole story, the one thing that never changes, never shifts its ground, is not affected or turned aside by the waywardness and rebellion of the son? Surely it is the father's love. Thus, even in the far country, away from the father and the father's house, that love was present, moving, moulding, guiding, drawing, till the time when the prodigal came home again.

The state of a sinner's life is not something which takes God unaware, just as the prodigal's home-coming was no surprise to the father. God does not first begin to know our needs when we present ourselves before him in penitence, seeking forgiveness and restoration. His love to us is an *antecedent love;* it is prior to and before any love on our part for him. How much the Scriptures teach us of the antecedence of the love of God! The Apostle John declares, for example: 'Beloved, let us love one another: for love is of God; and everyone that loveth is born of God, and knoweth God. He that loveth not knoweth not God; for God is love. In this was manifested the love of God toward us, because that God sent his only begotten Son into the world, that we might live through him. Herein is love, not that we loved God, but that he loved us, and sent his Son to be the propitiation for our sins' (1 John 4:7ff.). And later on in the same chapter we are told simply: 'We love him, because he first loved us' (v. 19).

Now, this love is not only prior in time. It is not merely as though God loved us in history before we came to love him: not as though he loved us already yesterday, and so we come to love him today. Rather, we are told that he loved us and set his name upon us and determined to save us even from before the creation of the world. 'He hath chosen us in him before the foundation of the world, that we should be holy and without blame before him' (Eph. 1:4). 'God hath from the beginning chosen you to salvation through sanctification of the Spirit and belief of the truth' (2 Thess. 2:13). God 'hath saved us, and called us with an holy calling, not according to our works, but according to his own purpose and grace, which was given us in Christ Jesus before the world began' (2 Tim. 1:9). 'And we know that all things work together for good to them that love God, to them who are the called according to his purpose. For whom he did foreknow, he also did predestinate to be conformed to the image of his Son, that he might be the firstborn among many brethren' (Rom. 8:28,29). These are only a few of the passages bearing upon the subject of the priority, the antecedence of God's love, but they will serve to show that the love of God is an eternal love, and that whatever love his people may have for him is grounded firmly and solely in the love he first had for them. What a great thing it is to know that the gospel is not something which originated in the recent past, which has its origins in the events of yesterday or the day before, but which is to be traced back all the way to the love of God for his own even before the first creative word was spoken and the world sprang into being as he lifted up his voice in omnipotent command!

The crown and glory of the gospel is that God's plan of salvation is an eternal plan, that the love he bears for us is an eternal love, that the compassion with which he regards us is an eternal compassion. The undergirding and over-arching principle from which the whole of Scripture draws its unity and force is the freeness, the sovereignty, the prevenience, the eternity of the grace of God.

It is no wonder that Augustus Toplady wrote:

> *The glory, Lord, from first to last,*
> *Is due to thee alone;*
> *Aught to ourselves we dare not take,*
> *Or rob thee of thy crown.*

The third great truth to be underscored with regard to the love of which we speak is that *it is not a passive thing*. There is nothing more striking and more important about the compassion of the Father than that it is active, seeking, and saving. It is not merely a mental attitude in which the Father feels sorrow for his son, or sympathizes with him in the sorry condition to which he has fallen. That would be a passive, ineffectual, ultimately meaningless definition of compassion. And though there is perhaps some consolation for us in knowing that others may share in our wretchedness, so that we are not altogether alone, yet such knowledge as that does not serve to lift us up out of our situation. The contrast here is between human help and divine. I do not suggest, of course, that our fellow human beings are incapable of doing anything for us. They most certainly can and do. There is no single one of us who has not benefited immeasurably from the comfort, and aid, and assistance, and guidance of others. What would you have been, for example, without your father and mother? or without some wise teacher? or without some generous friend? But I do insist that when it comes to eternal issues, to sin and judgment and condemnation, to the need for God's grace and forgiveness, to our disobedience and unworthiness over against God, then no human help, however well intended, however relatively wise and genuine, can be of any avail at all.

The glorious fact before us here is that the love of God is not merely theoretical, something that exists apart from the facts and events of history, but that it is an accomplishing, saving love. Those whom God pursues and seeks, he also finds and saves. 'Whither shall I go from thy spirit? or whither shall I flee from thy presence? If I ascend up into heaven, thou art there; if I make my bed in hell, behold, thou art there. If I take the wings of the morning, and dwell in the uttermost parts of the sea, even there shall thy hand lead me, and thy right hand shall hold me. If I say, Surely the darkness shall cover me, even the night shall be light about me. Yea, the darkness hideth not from thee; but the night shineth as the day: the darkness and the light are both alike to thee' (Ps. 139:7ff.). We are told, to be sure, that we must seek the Lord while he may be found, and call upon him while he is near (Is. 55:6f.), but even that is only possible because, seeking us, he has come upon us and found us and given us the will and desire to turn to him.

Surely the picture which Jesus gives us of the father bears out this truth. We see it in the response of the father to the appearance of his son. 'Bring forth the best robe, and put it on him; and put a ring on his hand, and shoes on his feet: and bring hither the fatted calf, and kill it; and let us eat, and be merry: for this my son was dead, and is alive again; he was lost, and is found.' And we must bear in mind that this reception and restoration of the son is only the final issue of the whole active work of the father in the son's behalf. The three parables in Luke 15 are all to be taken together and speak to a similiar effect. The shepherd leaves the ninety and nine sheep who are safe and goes after the one which is lost until he finds it and brings it home again. The woman ransacks her house till she has recovered the one coin of silver among ten that has been lost and put it back in its place. Just so does God seek that sheep of his, that treasure of his, that son of his, till he has come in—no, till he, actively, has made him to come in!

We have seen that there is in the parable, and in all the teaching of the New Testament, a contrast between human helplessness and the saving power of God. It is Christ who is the Saviour of his own. And I cannot too much stress the significance of this great reality. The offer of the gospel is certainly that: it is the offer of salvation upon the condition of repentance and faith; and it is to be preached freely and indiscriminately and to as many as possible. The church's commission to proclaim the redeeming work of Christ extends to 'all nations' (Matt. 28:19). But it is—thank God!—much more than an offer. What is presented to us in the Scriptures from the teachings of Christ and the apostles is not only the possibility of salvation, but its certainty for all those who are in Christ, for all those for whom he died.

This then is the truth in which alone we, like the prodigal, can find comfort. God is not only love but he *acts* upon that love. And his love is rooted, not in what we are, but in eternity. More, it is rooted in his own character. Why was it that the father so received such a son? Surely the answer is that what moved him was his own person and being. Just as that father, God loved and loves because he is loving, because he is love. Theologians sometimes speculate as to the attributes of God and whether any one of them may be raised above the others as more essential and more really descriptive of his essential being. Some have said that it is his 'otherness,' his transcendence, which is most God-like among his virtues and excellences. Others have suggested that God's holiness is to be lifted up above his other attributes as more nearly characteristic of his essence. Generally it is held that none, neither his eternity, nor his righteousness, nor his holiness, nor any other of the divine attributes, may be singled out for special elevation. I think I agree with that. God is all his perfections, and he is them equally. However, I do venture to say that if any one of the great qualities of God is more glorious than the others it is that instanced here. The love of God has vast deep roots because it is rooted in God himself and is, in one sense, his crowning glory and perfection. Wrathful he could have been against us; and wrathful he is against sin, and against impenitent sinners. But Christ has come, and come to make possible the covering over of our sins, the atonement—he is the propitiation for us through faith in his blood—in order that we should be his adopted brethren, the sons and daughters of God! It is not strange, then, that Henry Lyte with the fulness of Christian understanding could exclaim:

> *Praise, my soul, the King of heaven,*
> *To his feet thy tribute bring;*
> *Ransomed, healed, restored, forgiven,*
> *Who, like me, his praise should sing?*
> *Praise him! praise him!*
> *Praise the everlasting King!*

8. 'He Ran, and Fell on His Neck, and Kissed Him'

*W*e have already said a good deal about the compassion of God as it is pictured for us in the parable of the prodigal son, but we have to go one step further now. For while much that the Scriptures tell us of the divine pity has been adduced to show us clearly just what this love is, and in what it consists, yet the chief thing is so very important, so indispensable indeed, that if we omit it and leave the subject of God's compassion here, all the rest would be quite stripped of meaning. I have already suggested that there is a contrast in these parables of Luke 15 between the empty, impotent sympathy and compassion of mere men on the one hand, and the powerful, effectual, saving pity of God on the other. But it is not enough to speak only of the fact itself, as though we need know nothing more than that God is almighty and can fulfil his own word.

There is a school of interpretation which regards the parable of the prodigal son as in a sense a representation of the whole of the gospel. It is called the *evangelium in evangelio*, 'the gospel within the gospel.' The notion is defended that all the elements of the way of salvation are given us in it, that in fact we require nothing more than what the Saviour teaches here. The accent then would fall upon the free, gratuitous forgiveness of God, as though all he demanded were for the sinner to show himself sorrowful and penitent for what he had done in order for the remission of sins to take place. I do not doubt but that the picture of God on which this interpretation is based has been very widespread. God is conceived as kindly, gentle, beneficent, and merciful in the sense that, if there is the least sign of remorse or regret, he will never exact punishment for sin. Indeed, those who hold this genial image of God frequently go so far as to deny that God will ever punish anyone eternally, and to teach that the visitations and judgments of God in this world have no eternal counterpart, they are not foretastes of the wrath to come, but are all the punishment there is ever going to be. God rather—so they assure us—will eventually save all, in the end somehow having brought all to an acknowledgement of wrong-doing and of dependence upon him. But it is not true to say that God simply, gratuitously forgives sins, without payment of a price for them. Nor is it true to say that the whole gospel is included within the scope of the single parable of the prodigal son. And both ideas must be denied for the very same reason.

In that vision of God which was given on Mt. Sinai Moses heard the voice of God proclaim: ''The Lord, the Lord God, merciful and gracious, longsuffering, and abundant in goodness and truth, keeping mercy for thousands, forgiving iniquity and transgression and sin, and that will by no means clear the guilty; visiting the iniquity of the fathers upon the children, and upon the children's children, unto the third and to the fourth generation' (Exod. 34:6,7). Here we see the close juxtaposition of the Lord's grace and mercy on the one hand, and his refusal to clear the guilty on the other. The vast significance of that can scarcely be overestimated. God is gracious. Otherwise he would never have revealed himself in the Scriptures. He could very well have abandoned us to ourselves, left us to our own devices. We deserved nothing more. Instead, he chose, our own blindness and sin notwithstanding, to show us something of himself; and we know therefore, as the prophet tells us, that he delights in demonstrating mercy (Mic. 7:18). At the same time, however, his own justice and equity demand that sin be punished. The principle is laid down very early in the Bible that without the shedding of blood there is no remission of sins. And that great truth is continually reiterated throughout all the subsequent history of redemption. Sin is directed against God; sin takes upon itself an infinite character because committed against the infinite God; no penalty save the ultimate penalty of death can suffice to the eradicating of the crime and the guilt of sin. Hence, though it is in the Old Testament that we are told that the Lord is merciful, gracious, longsuffering, abundant in goodness and truth, it is also in the Old Testament that we are reminded time and again by the sacrifices of blood in the tabernacle first of all, and then afterward in the temple itself, of the capital nature of sin, that its blotting out can only be accomplished by death.

That leads us to say—and here we have the epitome of the expression of the divine compassion—that all the animals slain under the law as an element in the worship of the Old Testament were pointers, signs along the roadway, symbols, types, and that they all had one single reference in the end. The hymnwriter, Isaac Watts, caught this when he wrote:

> *Not all the blood of beasts*
> *On Jewish altars slain,*
> *Could give the guilty conscience peace,*
> *Or wash away the stain.*

They lacked authority, power, efficacy in themselves—those countless thousands of lambs and kids and heifers of Levitical worship! But they did one thing. Or rather, they did two things, which were really one. They gave clear expression to the seriousness of sin. And they pointed to the ultimate remedy for sin which would one day be provided. To those who object that the service of God in the Old Testament (and for that matter in the New, with its central doctrine of the atonement) is nothing but an abattoir, or slaughterhouse religion, one may reply that by calling it such they reveal within themselves a gravely defective understanding of what sin is. What is indeed repulsive in the sacrificial system is the sin which made it necessary. The fault is not with God and the manner in which he has commanded men to worship him, but with sinners. The fearful thing about the shedding of blood in the worship of God in the Old Testament administration was not the savagery of the act itself, but the sinfulness of the men and women who had to come before the Lord in this way if they were to come at all. And the best, or worst, was yet to be. Isaac Watts, who sang of the impotence of the blood of beasts slain on Jewish altars, went on to write:

> *But Christ, the heav'nly Lamb,*
> *Takes all our sins away,*
> *A sacrifice of nobler name*
> *And richer blood than they.*

Those animal sacrifices of Old Testament times all pointed to Calvary and to the blood of his cross; and when he came, they were all done away. They were rendered unnecessary because they had been fulfilled.

Now what, we may ask, does the cross of Christ mean? How can it be introduced in connection with the so beautiful and so affecting parable of the prodigal son? The reason is not far to seek. I have said that the whole gospel is not to be found within the quite narrow limits of this single parable. We must set it in its proper context. We must understand what Christ is doing here. And we must above all remember that it is he who tells it. When the father saw his son, he had compassion on him. The precise meaning of that statement, so far as its reference to God is concerned, is that the Father, the heavenly Father, has so great compassion, so great pity, so great mercy, as not even to spare his own Son in accomplishing the salvation of his prodigal sons and daughters. That is the teaching of the Word of God. That is the gospel. 'For God so loved the world, that he gave his only begotten Son, that whosoever believeth in him should not perish, but have everlasting life' (John 3:16). 'For when we were yet without strength, in due time Christ died for the ungodly. For scarcely for a righteous man will one die: yet peradventure for a good man some would even dare to die. But God commendeth his love toward us, in that, while we were yet sinners, Christ died for us' (Rom. 5:6,7,8). 'And all things are of God, who hath reconciled us to himself by Jesus Christ, and hath given to us the ministry of reconciliation; to wit, that God was in Christ, reconciling the world unto himself, not imputing their trespasses unto them; and hath committed unto us the word of reconciliation. Now then we are ambassadors for Christ, as though

God did beseech you by us: we pray you in Christ's stead, be ye reconciled to God. For he hath made him to be sin for us, who knew no sin; that we might be made the righteousness of God in him' (2 Cor. 5:18-21).

You see, the compassion of God is so seeking, so reconciling, so all-encompassing, so entire, so effective, so accomplishing, that in acting upon it he did not even spare his own Son, but, as the Apostle Paul says, 'delivered him up for us all' (Rom. 8:32). What a difference between this understanding of compassion which sees its highest expression in the cross of Calvary and that other which regards it merely as a sympathetic, pitying mental attitude and little more! Our God is a *saving* God. The gospel we preach is a gospel, not of potential salvation, of salvation rendered possible, but of salvation in fact and in deed. Do you wish to know what God is like? Then look at the cross of his Son. There in all its horror and cruelty and viciousness and corruption sin has been judged and put to death. There the debt of my sin has been paid. There the spotless Lamb of God took away the sin of the world. There he, even Jesus, was 'set forth to be a propitiation through faith in his blood' (Rom. 3:25). There salvation was not only enabled, brought near to realization, the way opened for men and women to come to God, but it was actually effected and brought to pass. Jesus Christ died, as the highest and fullest manifestation of God's compassion for sinners, in order to save his people from their sins.

You see, thus, what it means to read and to believe and to depend upon those words: 'But when he was yet a great way off, his father saw him, and had compassion, and ran, and fell on his neck, and kissed him.'

Before we leave this great truth there is one further vital lesson to be drawn from this stage in the prodigal son's experience. It is a lesson which shows us who the persons are toward whom this love of God, manifest in Christ, is directed. We have already seen that there was no causal bond between the son's evident need and the father's emotion of compassion. That compassion was not born in a moment's time when the prodigal at long last made his appearance on the roadway leading to the father's house. It had existed from the first, and was only awaiting this opportunity for expressing itself. But the time when that love was manifested shows us that *the compassion of the Father has its focus on penitents.*

To make this clear I have only to indicate how different the situation would have been had the son come home again, whether needy or not, in the same arrogant, self-sufficient frame of mind as that in which he set out. Had he done so, the father would still have loved him, just as he loved him when he showed himself bent upon a life of indulgence and sin. But it could hardly have been written that he 'ran, and fell on his neck, and kissed him,' and said to his servants, 'Bring forth the best robe, and put it on him; and put a ring on his hand, and shoes on his feet: and bring hither the fatted calf, and kill it; and let us eat, and be merry: for this my son was dead, and is alive again; he was lost, and is found.' All that presupposes the son to have come home in a manner quite different from that in which he left it. And the pity and mercy and compassion of God are not without focus and direction, as though every man, no matter what his attitude and what his spirit, were their object.

One remembers those awful words of Jesus which he

addressed to the scribes and Pharisees, those who thought themselves healthy and whole and in no need of a physician: 'Woe unto you, scribes and Pharisees, hypocrites! for ye make clean the outside of the cup and of the platter, but within they are full of extortion and excess. . . . Woe unto you, scribes and Pharisees, hypocrites! for ye are like unto whited sepulchres, which indeed appear beautiful outward, but are within full of dead men's bones, and of all uncleanness. Even so ye also outwardly appear righteous unto men, but within ye are full of hypocrisy and iniquity. Woe unto you, scribes and Pharisees, hypocrites! because ye build the tombs of the prophets, and garnish the sepulchres of the righteous, and say, If we had been in the days of our fathers, we would not have been partakers with them in the blood of the prophets. Wherefore ye be witnesses unto yourselves, that ye are the children of them which killed the prophets. Fill ye up then the measure of your fathers. Ye serpents, ye generation of vipers, how can ye escape the damnation of hell?' (Matt. 23:25-33). And lest it be thought that the wrath of God is only directed toward the impenitently and apparently irremediably self-righteous, I remind you of those terrible words of condemnation from the first chapter of Paul's Epistle to the Romans where he deals with the fearful immorality and ungodliness of his time: 'Because that, when they knew God, they glorified him not as God, neither were thankful, . . . Wherefore God also gave them up to uncleanness through the lusts of their own hearts, to dishonour their own bodies between themselves.' And then, after giving a list of appalling sins of which many among his contemporaries had made themselves guilty, the Apostle concludes: 'Who knowing the judgment of God, that they which commit such things are worthy of death, not only do the same, but have pleasure in them that do them' (Rom. 1:24-32).

I cannot stress too strongly that the receiving, forgiving, restoring love and compassion of God are reserved for *penitent* sinners, not for those who press on unashamedly and unabashedly in their defiance of the righteous commandments of God. The distinction between the saved and the lost is also the distinction between the penitent and the impenitent, between those who come to God through Jesus Christ, forsaking their sins, and those who continue in their wickedness, never asking, never wanting to ask, that question which is greater than all other questions: 'What must I do to be saved?'

There is a school of thought abroad at the present time which teaches the notion that all will be redeemed in the end, no matter what they do, no matter whether or not they take refuge in the blood of Christ's cross. It claims that Christ died for all without distinction, and that he in fact accomplished the redemption of all. Hence, even those who know nothing of Christ, or who wilfully persist in rejecting the gospel, will be brought to salvation one day, their own stubborn refusal to turn notwithstanding. The object of missions is identified by those who think along these lines as preaching to, telling all men and women that Christ died for them, and that they are his and included in his plan of redemption, whether they know it or not, whether they are indifferent to it or not. But there is no single shred of evidence in the Word of God for any such fancy as this. Rather the reverse! We are told clearly that 'there is none other name under heaven given among men, whereby we must be saved,' no other name than the name of Jesus (Acts 4:12). The Apostle Paul, in his sermon on Mars' Hill in

Athens, preaching as he is to the most learned and most cultivated men and women of his time, men and women who knew philosophy and religion, was careful to say that God 'now commandeth all men every where to repent: because he hath appointed a day, in the which he will judge the world in righteousness by that man whom he hath ordained; whereof he hath given assurance unto all men, in that he hath raised him from the dead' (Acts 17:30,31). He was speaking, of course, of the Lord Jesus Christ. In the Gospel of John we are told very plainly: 'He that believeth on the Son hath eternal life; but he that obeyeth not the Son shall not see life, but the wrath of God abideth on him' (3:36, ASV). And the Saviour himself quite settled the matter when he said in those beautiful but awesome words: 'I am the way, the truth, and the life: no man cometh unto the Father, but by me' (John 14:6).

You see thus the link between the penitence of the sinner, and the exercise of divine compassion. I do not say that there is any sense in which the sinner may be said to merit or earn the goodness of God. Even in the instance of the prodigal son, it was the father's caring, and the father's love, and the father's constancy, and the father's seeking, which at last brought him home again. This is not said in so many words in the passage with which we are concerned now, but it is altogether apparent in the other two parables of Luke 15. It was the seeking of the shepherd that restored the lost sheep. It was the seeking of the woman that found the lost coin. Just so is it—for these parables are to be taken together and speak to a similar effect—the seeking of the father which brings the son back home again and restores him to sonship. But God has his own way of dealing with us. And it is not as proud, self-sufficient, self-righteous, independent beings that we are made citizens of the kingdom of heaven, but as penitents, in the same manner and along the same pathway as the prodigal son.

As the father saw his son in that condition, and immediately perceived his new attitude and his genuine, deep-seated, thorough-going repentance, all the tenderness and pity and compassion and mercy that had moved him through the weary years of separation and waiting now welled up within him. And loving him, and yearning over him, he received him and forgave him.

> *How blest is he whose trespass*
> *Has freely been forgiv'n,*
> *Whose sin is wholly covered*
> *Before the sight of heaven.*
> *Blest he to whom Jehovah*
> *Will not impute his sin,*
> *Who has a guileless spirit,*
> *Whose heart is true within.*
>
> *While I kept guilty silence*
> *My strength was spent with grief,*
> *Thy hand was heavy on me,*
> *My soul found no relief;*
> *But when I owned my trespass,*
> *My sin hid not from thee,*
> *When I confessed transgression,*
> *Then thou forgavest me.*

(Psalm 32)

Such is the way of God's grace. And even more clearly than in the thirty-second Psalm is the mercy of God represented in this parable. You see here that the Father's compassion anticipated and preceded the son's expression of grief and shame because of his sin. 'When he was yet a great way off,' before he had opportunity to say a single word of the speech he had already prepared in the far country, 'his father saw him, and had compassion, and ran, and fell on his neck, and kissed him.'

How grateful I am for this truth! When someone comes to me with a broken life and a long history of sin, in bondage to his own lusts and wickedness but longing to be free, I am very glad indeed to know and to be able to tell him that while he cannot save himself, and though he may not have it in him to roll back the tide of years that has washed over him, yet there is mercy and compassion with the Lord for all who come to him.

There you are, my friend, perhaps in the very same position as this young man. Your conscience troubles you night and day. You put a good face on things before your family and friends. But within there is a gnawing, fretting, aching pain of spirit, because you know that if this day should be your last you are still without hope and without God in the world. Nevertheless, your sins do trouble you, and you long for something better, something that can satisfy the emptiness inside you, that can cut out the unrestraint and indiscipline and lust within you. You want peace, and have till now never been able to find it. You want God, but have not known how to or where to seek for him, and you have been afraid, ashamed it may be, to ask. I tell you now that the Lord has spoken and recorded this story for you, and for all others like you, and by it he encourages you to come. What have you to offer him? How will you excuse yourself? Is there any justification you can offer for wasted years and mis-spent opportunity? There is nothing to be said in answer to any of these questions, but this: Come as the prodigal came! Come, not arguing and pleading anything of your own, but only the cross of Christ.

9. 'And They Began to Be Merry'

*T*hus far a parallel has been clear enough between Christ's parable of the prodigal son and much human experience. We may find in human relationships at least something resembling the love with which the father welcomed home his lost son, faint and utterly inadequate though any comparison with the love of God must be. But the parable now reaches a point at which no correspondence can exist between the spiritual truth of the parable and any merely human story.

Parents today may witness with joy the return of children who, it may be, have wasted years. They can indeed know the relief of seeing a separation ended which they feared might last for ever, the joy of finding that an estrangement was not irremediable, and that the wrecked life of one who meant so much to them can be put together again. To this point we can certainly enter into the father's feelings in the story of Christ's parable. We understand how his mind would be eased, and how he would be thankful to see his son coming home.

For any father or mother the thought of a son, a

daughter, who has gone astray must often be too much to bear, and one can only live with something like that by making the necessary mental adjustments, learning to put it out of one's mind, deliberately refusing to dwell upon it. Such parents must often have thoughts very much akin to those of Jacob who, discerning (we may think) something of the crookedness and corruption in his family that had caused him to be bereft of Joseph and refusing to be comforted, said, 'For I will go down into the grave unto my son mourning.' And we are told, 'Thus his father wept for him' (Gen. 37:35). When a change for the better comes about, therefore, and there is repentance, turning, a restoration of broken relationships; when it seems that a child has determined at long last to mend his ways; it is a self-evident thing that a father's heart will be uplifted.

Yet alongside such feelings of joy in human experience there is also something else which remains. The sad truth is that there is something irreparable about damage done to human lives through disruptive, wilful waywardness, and that when parents have a prodigal child restored to them, though they will feel relief and gladness and a certain joy, yet that joy can never be entirely full, simply because the past can never be entirely undone. The bitterness brought by mis-spent years—years of rebellion and disobedience and disappointment and sin—is not wholly drained away even when reconciliation occurs. Regrets can remain, and recollections may arise which retain the power of causing anguish.

As a minister I have seen what such experiences can do to parents. I have a vivid recollection of a case in which a young husband and father left his family behind him, disappearing without a trace of any kind. To this day he has never been heard from again. The wife he deserted suffered terribly, and the family will always bear the scars of that abandonment. I think, however, that the old father and mother suffered most of all. One could never come into their home and take up any conversation with them without the puzzle and agony of this wayward son's misconduct being raised. All the rest of their days life was overshadowed by the mystery and unreason and prodigalness of the beloved son, and they went to their grave still mourning and longing and yearning over that long since vanished boy. What a relief to them it would have been had he written them a letter, called them on the telephone, let them know he was alive, regretful, sorry, prepared even to take up the tangled threads of his life with them again. But all they had was silence, a silence so complete it was almost as though the son were dead. Suppose, however, that he had come back, had repented, had begun anew. What then? They would, of course, with gladness and relief have received him back again, and given thanks to God. They would also, I think, have given him a place in their home and family, a place he had deliberately repudiated and scorned. But the scar, the shame, the shadow would have remained.

We all know the longing of words such as these:

> *Backward, turn backward, O time, in your flight,*
> *Make me a child again just for to-night!*
> *Mother, come back from the echo-less shore,*
> *Take me again to your heart as of yore;*
> *Kiss from my forehead the furrows of care,*
> *Smooth the few silver threads out of my hair;*
> *Over my slumbers your loving watch keep;—*
> *Rock me to sleep, Mother—rock me to sleep!*
> *(Elizabeth Akers Allen)*

How much more then the prodigal sons and daughters among us! But whether our fathers and mothers live or not, there is no backward movement of time, no recalling of days that are past, no undoing the deeds that are done.

I said at the outset that we have reached the point in the parable where the spiritual truth taught wholly diverges from human experience. What is so striking in the words to which we now come is that they show that the father, when his son comes back to him, has more than relief, more than gladness, more than joy tinged with regret for those wasted years. The father, and therefore the son also, *has fulness of joy.* 'When he was yet a great way off, his father saw him, and had compassion, and ran, and fell on his neck, and kissed him.' Those words give us the man's immediate response. And then afterwards he exclaimed, 'This my son was dead, and is alive again; he was lost, and is found,' and the whole company 'began to be merry.' The Lord Jesus is calling our attention to the joy with which the father welcomes and receives his son.

That joy is a marvellous thing! It is true we can understand *something* of it, the story being so true to life, but the more-than-human in it, the divine in it, that which radically differentiates between this parable and our ordinary human experience, is quite beyond our ken.

The Scriptures tell us many things about God. They are his self-revelation, and all we know for certain about him we know because he has said it of himself in his own Word. It is the Scriptures which are able to make us 'wise unto salvation through faith which is in Christ Jesus' (2 Tim. 3:15). And it is the Scriptures which are given by inspiration of God, and are profitable for doctrine, reproof, correction, instruction in righteousness (2 Tim. 3:16). We learn in them that 'God is a Spirit, infinite, eternal, unchangeable, in his being, wisdom, power, holiness, justice, goodness, and truth' (*Shorter Catechism*, Q. 4). We are told in the Bible of God's eternal plan of salvation, begun already before the foundation of the world, carried out with increasing degrees of clarity in the Old Testament period, fulfilled in the person and work of our Lord Jesus Christ. The Scriptures are full of the mercy and grace, the love and compassion of God. 'The Lord is merciful and gracious, slow to anger, and plenteous in mercy. He will not always chide: neither will he keep his anger for ever. He hath not dealt with us after our sins; nor rewarded us according to our iniquities. For as the heaven is high above the earth, so great is his mercy toward them that fear him. As far as the east is from the west, so far hath he removed our transgressions from us. Like as a father pitieth his children, so the Lord pitieth them that fear him' (Ps. 103:8-13). All the excellences of God are glorious beyond human understanding, and in every one of his virtues and attributes he is infinite perfection. 'God is light, and in him is no darkness at all' (1 John 1:5).

But while all these truths, as we have seen, are wonderfully confirmed in this parable, the words of Jesus to which we have now come reveal something more which is new and different. New and different in the sense that this emphasis on the *joy of God in the repentance of sinners*—found in all three parables which make up this fifteenth chapter of Luke's Gospel—is not everywhere accentuated or even alluded to as it is here, and that we do not ordinarily think in such terms with respect to God.

Consider for a moment the two parables which precede the one we are studying. You remember the parable of the shepherd with the hundred sheep, one of which becomes lost. Jesus tells us that he leaves the ninety-nine in order to go after that which is lost, till he finds it, and then, so we read, 'he layeth it on his shoulders, *rejoicing*. And when he cometh home, he calleth together his friends and neighbours, saying unto them, *Rejoice* with me; for I have found my sheep which was lost.' Whereupon the Saviour adds the conclusion: 'I say unto you, that likewise *joy* shall be in heaven over one sinner that repenteth, more than over ninety and nine just persons, which need no repentance.' Think, furthermore, of the second parable in this same chapter about the woman who has ten pieces of silver, one of which is lost to her. She is said to light a candle and to sweep the house and to seek diligently till she finds it. And when the lost coin has been restored to her again, so the story runs, 'she calleth her friends and her neighbours together, saying, *Rejoice* with me; for I have found the piece which I had lost.' And again, Christ adds a conclusion and an interpretation: 'Likewise I say unto you, there is *joy* in the presence of the angels of God over one sinner that repenteth.'

Now once more, in the parable with which we are especially concerned, the Lord Jesus Christ is revealing to us, is stressing, the joy of God in the salvation of sinners. The chapter is one of great beauty, and fairly reverberates with the note of joy to be found throughout it. We have already observed that the first and second parables end with a refrain in which the joy of heaven at the salvation of the sinner comes to expression. This is even more clearly the case with the third. Twice over, at the conclusion of the first part of the story which has to do with the prodigal and his return and again at the conclusion of the second, in which we find the response of the elder brother, the father is represented as declaring in a voice surely vibrant with the highest and holiest and most perfect of joys: 'For this my son was dead, and is alive again; he was lost, and is found'' (vv. 24 and 32).

What a voice that is, a voice pregnant with heavenly joy! It is the Father's voice, God's voice, uplifted in a cry which echoes and re-echoes backward to the eternal past even before the foundation of the world when our redemption was already fixed in the sovereign purpose of God, and forward to the unending future when all his ransomed prodigals, found and brought home at last, shall dwell with him and reign with him and rejoice with him and sing his praises in the new heaven and the new earth!

Had you thought of God in such terms as these? I fear very much that even most Christians have an altogether too passive picture of God in their minds. They love him for what he has done in their behalf. They praise him for his saving power. They give thanks for sins forgiven and for the life he promises and pledges to them. But they do not think of him as feeling, as being involved, as sorrowful and grieving because of sin, as full of joy and gladness upon the repentance of sinners. If that is your attitude, then you have greatly misunderstood him. Think again of that marvellous statement from the Old Testament: 'Who is a God like unto thee, that pardoneth iniquity, and passeth by the transgression of the remnant of his heritage? he retaineth not his anger for ever, because he *delighteth in mercy*' (Mic. 7:18). God, says the prophet, is incomparable and all-glorious in all respects, but in this also and in this chiefly, that he rejoices in the demonstration of mercy.

If this is so—and we have the word of our Lord Jesus Christ for it—then you may know what a welcome there is for penitent, believing sinners! The Scriptures insist upon the truth that to be gracious, to forgive sins, is the activity in which God takes the greatest pleasure. 'As I live, saith the Lord God, I have no pleasure in the death of the wicked; but that the wicked turn from his way and live: turn ye from your evil ways; for why will ye die, O house of Israel?' (Ezek. 33:11). God takes no delight in the inevitable sentence of death upon the impenitently wicked. His joy is in welcoming the prodigal back home again. 'God, who is rich in mercy, for his great love wherewith he loved us, even when we were dead in sins, hath quickened us together with Christ' (Eph. 2:4,5). 'And they began to be merry.'

And yet we must also say that in a very real sense this attitude of God's is hard to understand. It is both difficult and astonishing. Consider only the unworthiness of the objects of his mercy. Surely we must then ask ourselves why it is that God finds joy in saving them. Why should he who is altogether righteous and holy, who inhabits eternity, why should he who is God and in whom dwells no imperfection or impurity at all, show mercy to creatures who have rebelled against him, who continue to defy him, and who seem to find their greatest pleasure in trampling under foot his perfect Word? Those who have experienced a genuine conviction of sin are struck with a sense of awe and wonder at the mercy of God. They know—they who have sat as Paul sat in his Damascus room three days and three nights in the darkness of his blind eyes and misery, and now at last conscious estrangement from God and just condemnation under the demands of his holy law—what it means for God to love them and to show mercy towards them (Acts 9). How can it then be that there is joy in heaven over one sinner who repents? How shall we comprehend that the all-holy and all-righteous One can delight to draw sinful men and women to himself?

John Calvin, the great Genevan Reformer, gives us some glimpse of his own experience of these things in a precious fragment of what may well be autobiography—one of the few hints we have of the nature of his own spiritual pilgrimage—in his *Letter to Sadolet*. 'Every time that I looked within myself,' he writes in prayer to God, 'or raised my heart to Thee, so violent a horror overtook me that there were neither purifications nor satisfactions which could in any way cure me. The more I gazed at myself the sharper were the pricks which pressed my conscience, to such a point that there remained no other solace or comfort than to deceive myself by forgetting myself.' This state of affairs continued until he came to comprehend the mercy of God in the Lord Jesus Christ. 'And when my mind,' he goes on, 'had been made to be truly attentive I began to understand, as if someone had brought me a light, in what a mire of error I had wallowed, and had become filthy, and with how much mud and dirt I had been defiled. Being then grievously troubled and distracted, as was my duty, on account of the eternal death which hung over me, I judged nothing more necessary to me after having condemned with groanings and tears my past manner of life, than to give myself up and to partake myself to Thy way.' His reticent manner of expression makes this testimony of the Reformer even more powerful than it would have been had he gone into detail. It is clear, however, that he labored under a tremendous sense of unworthiness and the heavy burden of his sin.

How, it must be asked again, shall we grasp that God should delight to draw sinners to himself? Calvin could not comprehend it, nor could Luther, nor could Augustine, nor could Paul, nor could the prodigal. We are not required to penetrate into the mystery of it. Eternity itself will be too short for that. We are only asked to accept it and to believe it, and to cast ourselves in the confidence of it upon the goodness of God!

I have suggested that God's attitude in this respect is hard to understand when we consider the unworthiness of the objects of his mercy. Surely the delight God takes in the showing of mercy, is a breath-taking, glorious, unexpected thing! But there is a factor here which points up even more powerfully the difficulty involved in what is told us by the Saviour of the rejoicing of God, and *that is the prohibitively high cost which it necessarily involves.* God himself, one would think, must have been deterred in the exercise of grace by the enormous price which must be paid if we were to be saved. You see, in order to save, and to forgive, God must send his Son, his only Son. For without him all other tokens of favor, all other promises of love and fellowship and forgiveness, would be empty and meaningless. Jesus Christ is the supreme instance of God's mercy, and the One without whom and whose sacrifice there would be no mercy at all.

What a staggering thing it is that God should send his only begotten Son into the world 'in the likeness of sinful flesh, and for sin,' in order to put sin to death in the flesh (Rom. 8:3)! There is such a tremendous intrinsic improbability here that the mind staggers under the necessity of having to believe it. And yet the sublime thing is that this really happened, that it is so. Nothing else would do.

> *There was no other good enough*
> *To pay the price of sin;*

He only could unlock the gate
Of heav'n and let us in.

(Cecil Frances Alexander)

Of course, we are not told the details of this grand necessity in the parable of the prodigal son. The whole gospel, as we have said, is not given us here, but only certain aspects of it. Hints are not wanting, however. In reading the story one cannot help but sense something of the father's pain at the waywardness of the boy; and it cost him a great deal in terms of his own mind and spirit to show compassion and love when the son came home again. Still further, in the first of these three parables in Luke 15 something comes through to us of the pain and the anguish and the self-denial of that good shepherd's quest for his lost sheep. Elizabeth Clephane captures something of the pathos of the story:

'Lord, thou hast here thy ninety and nine;
Are they not enough for thee?'
But the Shepherd made answer, 'This of mine
Has wandered away from me,
And although the road be rough and steep,
I go to the desert to find my sheep.'

But none of the ransomed ever knew
How deep were the waters crossed;
Nor how dark was the night that the Lord passed thro'
Ere he found his sheep that was lost.
Out in the desert he heard its cry—
Sick and helpless, and ready to die.

'Lord, whence are those blood-drops all the way
That mark out the mountain's track?'
'They were shed for one who had gone astray
Ere the Shepherd could bring him back.'
'Lord, whence are thy hands so rent and torn?'
'They're pierced tonight by many a thorn.'

Though nothing is said here specifically of the cost to the Father of the prodigal's redemption, yet when we look at the whole teaching of the Scriptures there can be no question about the vastness of the price which he paid. God did not spare his own Son, the Apostle Paul declares, 'but delivered him up for us all' (Rom. 8:32). 'For he hath made him to be sin for us, who knew no sin; that we might be made the righteousness of God in him' (2 Cor. 5:21). Christ Jesus, 'being in the form of God, thought it not robbery to be equal with God; but made himself of no reputation, and took upon him the form of a servant, and was made in the likeness of men: and being found in fashion as a man, he humbled himself, and became obedient unto death, even the death of the cross' (Phil. 2: 6-8). 'Surely he hath borne our griefs, and carried our sorrows: yet we did esteem him stricken, smitten of God, and afflicted. But he was wounded for our transgressions, he was bruised for our iniquities: the chastisement of our peace was upon him; and with his stripes we are healed' (Is. 53:4,5). Of the Lord Jesus Christ God said, 'This is my beloved Son, in whom I am well pleased' (Matt. 17:5). And yet, to save prodigals, 'it pleased the Lord to bruise him; he hath put him to grief' (Is. 53:10). And then think, too, of that awful hour, than which in all the history of the world there has never been a point of time more fraught with eternal consequences, more obscured in tremendous mystery, when the Son of God, the Second Person in the Trinity, the brightness of the Father's glory and the express image of his person, utterly deserted in his agony of hellish loneliness and isolation, cried out, 'My God, my God, why hast thou forsaken me?' That was the price that had to be paid for showing mercy. And yet so immense is the love of God, so much does he will to save, that, as the Apostle teaches us, God himself set forth his own Son, the Lord Jesus Christ, to be the sacrifice for sin, the means of propitiation, whereby his eternal justice could be satisfied and he also be at the same time the justifier of those that believe in the Saviour (Rom. 3:25,26).

How, we ask ourselves, how can it be that the Lord delights in mercy? How can there be joy in heaven over one repenting sinner? How, indeed, when the cost was the very life and soul of the only One who was in himself holy, harmless, undefiled, separate from sinners (Heb. 7:26)?

> *And can it be, that I should gain*
> *An interest in the Saviour's blood?*
> *Died He for me, who caused His pain—*
> *For me, who Him to death pursued?*
> *Amazing love! how can it be*
> *That Thou, my God, shouldst die for me?*
>
> *Tis mystery all! The Immortal dies:*
> *Who can explore His strange design?*
> *In vain the first-born seraph tries*
> *To sound the depths of love divine.*
> *'Tis mercy all! let earth adore,*
> *Let angel minds inquire no more.*
>
> *(Charles Wesley)*

O no, we cannot explain! Not when we remember our own sins and the curse due to us for them. Certainly not when we think of the infinite price paid for our redemption, when the Father sent the Son to die in the place of the prodigal! But our inability to explain does not annul the truth with which we are concerned. Nor does it in any sense reduce the magnitude of our awe and wonder. Rather, our helplessness in the face of the divine mercy, and the divine delight in mercy, must have the effect of impressing upon us with still greater force the glory of the saving work of God.

We must go on finally to say something of what this joy means in practical terms, what expression it finds, in the parable and in the lives of believers. The father's demonstration of joy at the prodigal's return we have already noticed. What has still to be considered is how immediately the father also *restores him to sonship.* You see in the parable that the son, moved surely by this outpouring of feeling on the part of his father, begins to speak the words which he had so carefully prepared and rehearsed in the far country. 'Father,' he says, 'I have sinned against heaven, and in thy sight, and am no more worthy to be called thy son.' But before he has opportunity to finish what he intended saying, the father breaks in, as though not having heard a single word of it, and cries out to the servants standing about and looking on at this reunion, 'Bring forth the best robe, and put it on him; and put a ring on his hand, and shoes on his feet: and bring hither the fatted calf, and kill it; and let us eat, and be merry: for this my son was dead, and is alive again; he was lost, and is found.' It was not, of course, that the father had no appreciation for the new humility his son had learned, for the repentance which had come to him after those long, dreary, punishing days in the land of his grief. Not the least part of his joy was certainly founded upon the fact that the son had returned a different man from the arrogant, self-confident youth who had set out from home to make his way in the world. It is a self-evident thing that the father was glad and full of gratitude for the transformation that had come over the boy. No, he did not interrupt the son's expression of penitence because he had no time for it and was unsympathetic toward it.

The reason why the father refused to permit his son to continue in that carefully prepared speech of his was that what the son proposed he could in no respect take into serious consideration. The prodigal wanted to say, 'Make me as one of thy hired servants.' The father said instead, 'This my son was dead, and is alive again; he was lost, and is found.'

You see the remarkable contrast here, the antithesis really: on the one hand, the purpose of the son to request a servant's place in the household of the father; on the other hand, the deliberate declaration on the part of the father that his son, though a wastrel and a prodigal, was a son even so. And upon that declaration the father at once proceeded to act in that he restored the boy to sonship. The prodigal was given the best robe in place of his tattered rags; a fine ring was thrust upon his finger; well-made shoes were fitted to his feet; the fatted calf was slaughtered for the feast of celebration. All the tokens of that erring, wayward boy's belonging to the father, being a son of the father, were produced; and before the whole household, indeed, before the whole world as it were, the father owned him, restored him, took him to his heart. 'This my son was dead, and is alive again; he was lost, and is found.' There could be but one relationship in which that son stood to his father. How could he, a son, become as one of the hired servants? Though gone astray, he was in fact a son! And it was to a son's place that he must be restored, if he were to be restored at all.

There are no two classes of people amongst those whom God is pleased to have in his family. Some have been tempted to think in such terms as these, and have distinguished between ordinary Christians on the one side and those living a higher, perhaps, celibate, ascetic, monastic life on the other; or between carnal, non-victorious Christians on the one side, and triumphant, victorious Christians on the other; that is, between those who, it is alleged, know Christ only as Saviour, and those who know him both as Saviour and as Lord. But the Word of God and the nature of the redemptive work of Christ leave no room for doubt in the matter. Christ is both Saviour and Lord for all his people. Similarly, there are no two classes of Christians in the sense of those who live ordinary lives and those who give themselves to celibacy and asceticism, as though the latter were holier and more honouring and closer to God than the former. The Lord has no step-children, and all who are sons are sons in the fullest sense. Never can a child of God be a mere hired servant in his father's house.

That points up as clearly as can be the intensity of the joy God has in the saving and receiving of sinners. The measure of his delight in mercy may be found in his giving them this status. Here it is described in terms of restoration to sonship. Elsewhere it is called the adoption of sons. In both cases what is in view is the fact that though because of sin we all have forfeited the right to call God our Father in virtue of creation, yet he by his grace receives us again in Christ and makes us his sons and daughters, not now any longer upon the basis of mere nature, because he created us in his own image, but upon the eternally secure ground of his sovereign mercy. The Apostle Paul puts it this way in his Epistle to the Romans: 'For as many as are led by the Spirit of God, they are the sons of God. For ye have not received the spirit of bondage again to fear; but ye have received the Spirit of adoption, whereby we cry, Abba, Father' (8:14,15). And in another place: 'When the fulness of the time was come, God sent forth his Son, made of a woman, made under the law, to redeem them that were under the law, that we might receive the adoption of sons. And because ye are sons, God hath sent forth the Spirit of his Son into your hearts, crying, Abba, Father. Wherefore thou art no more a servant, but a son; and if a son, then an heir of God through Christ' (Gal. 4:4-7).

We shall surely never hear more glorious news than the truth at which we have sought to look in this chapter. There is *joy* in heaven over one sinner who repents! What! joy in heaven over the conversion of a son so prodigal as this? Yes, that is the teaching of the Word of God. That is the revelation God has given us of himself. That is how we may understand him to be. And what a transformation that brings into the whole of our lives! God forgives sins. God delights to forgive sins. God rejoices to forgive sins. More, God is intent that lost sinners should become, at once, upon their conversion, his sons and daughters! Certainly he is holy and just and will by no means clear the guilty (Exod. 34:7). But he himself in his infinite mercy and grace has provided the means by which sinners may be cleansed and made new, their debt cancelled and done away: in the blood of his own Son spilt at Calvary. And his delight is in that glorious, God-like work.

> *But all thro' the mountains, thunder-riv'n,*
> *And up from the rocky steep,*
> *There arose a glad cry to the gate of heav'n,*
> *'Rejoice! I have found my sheep!'*
> *And the angels echoed around the throne,*
> *'Rejoice, for the Lord brings back his own!'*

10. 'He Was Angry, and Would not Go in'

We have concluded the discussion of the first part—the chief part—of Jesus' parable of the prodigal son. But we have not yet quite finished with the parable as a whole. The story is divided into two unequal halves. The one has to do with the young man himself, his sin, his separation from the father, his repentance, and his restoration to sonship. The other is concerned with the elder of the two sons, the one who stayed at home. To be sure, when the parable of the prodigal son is mentioned, one immediately thinks of the younger of the two, the one with whom we have so far been occupied; in every man's mind it is *his* spiritual pilgrimage which forms the principal interest of the story. Yet the Lord Jesus Christ went on, after having portrayed for us the reunion of the prodigal and his father, to tell us something in these additional verses about the brother who stayed at home.

It is significant that these two at first glance utterly dissimilar brothers should be made to stand over against one another in the parable. There is, of course, very much the same sort of thing in all three of the parables which make up the fifteenth chapter of Luke's Gospel. In the first of them one finds the contrast of the single lost sheep on the one hand and the ninety and nine which had not gone astray on the other. In the second it is a question of nine pieces of silver safe and where they belong, as opposed to the one which had come to be lost. And, though the numbers involved are here greatly reduced, yet in the parable of the prodigal son the concern is with a lost son on the one side, and the elder brother on the other. All this points us back to the opening verses of the chapter which we examined at the beginning of our study: 'Then drew near unto him all the *publicans* and *sinners* for to hear him. And the *Pharisees* and *scribes* murmured, saying, This man receiveth sinners, and eateth with them' (Luke 15:1,2). What is Jesus doing here? He is in each instance saying something about Pharisees and scribes as well as about sinners. We have already discovered in large measure what the Saviour has to teach us about sinners and what he came to do for them. Now we have to go on to inquire what it is that he intended to say about the other category among his hearers: that is, the sheep safe in the fold, the coins which had not been lost, the son who was never a prodigal.

You will notice at once a great difference in the manner in which he speaks of the older of the two sons. In a much abbreviated form, he gives us a sketch of the life story of the prodigal. Somehow, though the details given us are so few, we seem to have the feeling that we know the young man and can enter into his experience. It is, after all, very like our own. Not so, however, with the elder brother. We were made aware at the very beginning, of course, that 'a certain man had *two* sons.' We have remembered all along that the prodigal was not the only son of his father. Yet nothing is said of the other son till the celebration of the younger brother's return had got well underway. He is kept out of the picture and only brought in again to serve as a kind of foil at the end. The transformation of the prodigal is made to stand out the more clearly still when contrasted with the ultimately graceless condition of the elder brother.

Nevertheless, though it be true that we are told almost nothing about the older of the two sons, it needs to be added that we do most certainly know something about him by implication. He is the outwardly just person, one of those ninety and nine who think themselves righteous and at home and in no position demanding repentance. He is one of those of whom Jesus spoke when he said: 'They that be whole need not a physician, but they that are sick . . . , for I am not come to call the righteous, but sinners to repentance' (Matt. 9:12,13). He is, in a word, a Pharisee. Remember that Jesus was speaking to Pharisees and scribes as well as to publicans and sinners. We use that word *Pharisee* in a negative manner. It conveys something distasteful to us. No one loves a Pharisee, in our understanding of the word. We find ourselves much more at home with the prodigal, whatever crimes he may have committed against his father, than we do with the elder brother. But we have given what is surely a very wrong connotation to the word. In the Palestine of Christ's day it not only meant the self-righteous hypocrite, the man who regarded himself as immeasurably holier than others and who paraded his religiosity before the world, being proud of nothing so much as of his superior standing before God. The Pharisee was very often an upright man, a man of substance, a pillar in his community, a man of integrity in his business relationships, a man who took his religious faith with great seriousness and put it into practice in every area of life. There was something very wrong indeed with the Pharisee, but it was not that he lacked honesty, or that he was immoral, or that he was insincere. And it is precisely to point up and to illustrate in as graphic a manner as possible what the real trouble was in the life of these Pharisees and scribes that the Lord Jesus added these verses to the parable of the prodigal son about the elder brother.

I very often think of this second part of the parable as exemplifying what may perhaps be called the *'catalytic effect of conversion.'* What is a catalyst? In the scientific sense a catalyst is a substance, a relatively small quantity of which can promote a chemical reaction without itself being permanently changed or lost. A catalyst induces a reaction in other chemical substances, it causes that reaction to come about, without itself being directly or permanently involved in the change. Obviously we are not interested here primarily in chemistry. My point is simply that in the second part of the parable a kind of non-chemical catalytic reaction is taking place. The one substance, the prodigal son in this case, produces a reaction in the other, the elder brother. And it is that reaction which matters in these verses.

You see what has happened here. Everything that the prodigal was, his elder brother was not. The prodigal, as we have seen, was a wastrel of a son, a spendthrift, an ingrate, an unnatural child who demanded the inheritance which would have been his upon his father's death in order that he could spend it now; and when he had that substance, he made off with it to the far country, beyond the reach, as he thought, of his father's knowledge and his father's restraining hand, to live as he pleased. Not till his inheritance was gone, and it was plain to see what a failure he had made of himself, did he make his way again to the father and the father's house. That was the course events had followed. And that was the only interpretation of them allowed by the mind of the elder brother. But now, here was the wretched fellow back again, received into the father's home and heart, as though nothing had happened, or in spite of all that had happened. To be sure, one hoped that the boy had learned his lesson, but why did he have to be welcomed so heartily? Could not his father have placed him on probation for a period of time to see whether he really had changed? And why, too, did the father give him presents, and do things for the worthless prodigal which had never been done for himself? Those words: 'This my son was dead, and is alive again; he was lost, and is found,' had no meaning for the elder brother, save to bring his resentment to a still higher pitch. We shall have to say more about these things later on. For the moment we see what it was that provoked such a reaction. It was the return of the prodigal, the return of a transformed, truly penitent, submissive, obedient son, all those wasted years notwithstanding, that pointed up the true condition of the heart of the elder brother.

As we come to discuss the relation of the younger son to his elder brother, or rather, the relation of them both to the father, it should be underscored that the prodigal was now bound to his father in a relationship of *the freest and most perfect grace*. Scarcely does it seem just that the younger of the two sons, who had been guilty of so much that was shameful and wicked, should receive such a joyous and festive reception at his father's hands, while the older remains in the cold, until one realizes what purpose the Lord Jesus Christ has in mind here. It is not the sin of the prodigal which finds countenance and approval from the father! By no means, and in no respect! As we have already seen, the whole thing must have struck the elder brother as very unfair indeed. It appeared to him almost as though the father were condoning the kind of life his brother had lived; certainly as though he were not treating it with sufficient seriousness. 'Lo,' he said, 'these many years do I serve thee, neither transgressed I at any time thy commandment; and yet thou never gavest me a kid, that I might make merry with my friends. But as soon as this thy son was come, which hath devoured thy living with harlots, thou hast killed for him the fatted calf' (vv. 29,30).

The truth is, however, that he quite missed the point. Or rather, he was altogether incapable in the nature of the case of perceiving what the point really was. There is no approval of sin here, no tendency to take it rather more lightly than it ought to be taken. The father cannot be accused of doing so. God certainly cannot be accused of doing so. Can anyone find a single line in the Scriptures which indicates that God is less than deadly serious about sin, and regards it as anything other than heinous and ugly, worthy of judgment and death? How could he when the cost of dealing with it was so incalculably high? No, it is not a question of sin treated as anything other than sin. It is rather a question of the displaying of the freest and fullest possible degree of sovereign grace. And that, the elder brother is utterly unable to understand.

To be sure, the prodigal is restored to sonship. But the accent falls upon the words: 'This my son was dead, and is alive again; he was lost, and is found.' Those words, twice repeated within the short compass of the parable, tell us volumes about what has occurred here. The prodigal is not given a son's place in the house of his father because of any residual claim of nature. He had come to the realization of having forfeited that long since. Remember the plea which issued from the penitent's heart: 'Father, I have sinned against heaven, and before thee, and am no more worthy to be called thy son: make me as one of thy hired servants.' The sonship to which he is raised when he returns home is not one he may grasp as by right, but is given to him only in virtue of the father's love and grace. What he receives—and I want to stress that word *receives*—is quite the reverse of what he deserves. He does not get it, therefore, because he deserves it, but only because he receives it as a free gift. Grace earned is no grace at all. If we only have what is due us by right we shall have no grace in the end. The true contrast here is not between a son who had wilfully turned aside from and abandoned his father's love and a son who had remained faithful and obedient and had therefore earned the benefits of that love. It is rather between the penitent prodigal who understood now his need of the Father's grace and the impenitent elder brother who saw himself in no such need at all.

The essence of true religion, the very heart of the faith of the Scriptures, is grace. Unless we understand that, unless we come to stand where the prodigal stood, whatever our personal histories may be, we have failed to grasp anything whatsoever of our own position and of the nature of spiritual truth.

> *By grace I'm saved, grace free and boundless;*
> *My soul, believe and doubt it not.*
> *Why stagger at this word of promise?*
> *Hath Scripture ever falsehood taught?*
> *Nay; then this word must true remain:*
> *By grace thou, too, shalt heav'n obtain.*

By grace! None dare lay claim to merit;
Our works and conduct have no worth.
God in his love sent our Redeemer,
Christ Jesus, to this sinful earth;
His death did for our sins atone,
And we are saved by grace alone.

By grace! O, mark this word of promise
When thou art by thy sins oppressed,
When Satan plagues thy troubled conscience,
And when thy heart is seeking rest.
What reason cannot comprehend
God by his grace to thee doth send.

By grace! This ground of faith is certain;
So long as God is true, it stands.
What saints have penned by inspiration,
What in his Word our God commands,
What our whole faith must rest upon,
Is grace alone, grace in his Son.

(Christian L. Scheidt)

I wonder whether you have come to that conviction. Perhaps the most difficult thing to get across to people is this very truth. One can teach and preach and expound and proclaim that salvation is by grace alone, and that apart from the pure and unmixed grace of God there is no hope for eternity; but afterward, if one asks even those who claim to be Christians what the basis for their hope is, the answer will often be: 'I believe in God. I do the best I can. I think all will be well for me in the end.' What the prodigal came to comprehend at last is still entirely strange to them, and they appear unable to take it in. Of course they are unable to take it in! The very character of salvation as by grace means that until God has established contact with us, until he gives us his own life, we are yet dead in our trespasses and sins, without spiritual life, without the capacity for perceiving the significance of the gospel.

This failure to understand, this incomprehension, this deadness of human nature is always present, always the final obstacle which stands in the way of sinners coming to Christ. But it is perhaps even more dangerous at the present time than in the past because the Christian faith has been radically redefined by many who profess to adhere to it. They have made it essentially a way of life, and go so far as to say that to be a Christian means to be Christ-like, to use the life of Christ as a moral pattern for our lives. Christianity to them is no longer a spiritual, a supernatural religion, but a religion whose application is to the problems and difficulties and injustices and broken relationships of human society, and very little more. Of course the Scriptures have a great deal to say about these things, but to make them the primary object of Christ's coming and Christ's death is to reverse the Lord's own teaching and to corrupt and distort the truth. An attack upon human problems and disrupted human relationships can never be divorced from an insistence upon the necessity of the creation of new life in us. We dare not ever shrug our shoulders in indifference to the appalling wretchedness, bondage, and injustice so apparent in our own society and throughout the world. But neither do we dare to suggest that social conditions can be transformed without reference to new creaturehood in the Lord Jesus Christ. The great necessity for any man or woman is to be born again in the biblical sense of the word. 'Except a man be born again,' said Jesus, 'he cannot see the kingdom of God' (John 3:3). Unless we are clear at this point we stand before God, not as redeemed prodigal sons and daughters, but as still unredeemed elder brothers and sisters, strangers, all our efforts notwithstanding, to the grace and power of Christ to save. The first thing, that which must have highest priority with us, is to be converted to God.

We have observed that the prodigal son upon his return home and restoration to sonship was now bound to his father in a relationship of the freest and most perfect grace. Now as we examine the elder brother and his attitude more closely, it becomes plain that, if the prodigal was bound by grace to his father, the elder brother was bound to him—in his own view and by his own desire—*not in a relationship of grace, but in one of legal obligation.* The terms of the contrast are very clear indeed. The prodigal sees himself a son by grace; the elder brother a son by law. The prodigal sees himself as having done nothing to merit his sonship; the elder brother is quite convinced of his having earned everything the father has to give. The prodigal sees salvation as by nothing other than the mercy of God; the elder brother bases all upon sheer obedience and keeping the commandments of God.

It may seem hard at first glance to speak so severely of the elder brother as Christ does, and as we are forced to do. His record is vastly better than that of the prodigal. After all, he never demanded his inheritance from his father. He never went off to the far country and wasted his father's substance with riotous living. He never set himself deliberately against his father's will or challenged his father's authority. There is no reason to believe that he spoke anything other than the simple truth when he said of himself, 'Lo, these many years do I serve thee, neither transgressed I at any time thy commandment.' He was, at least outwardly, a good, steady, faithful son to his father, and had given no cause for reproof or alarm. Nor is it enough for us to condemn him over against his brother because of his self-righteousness. It is not as though Jesus were saying that the admittedly good conduct of the elder son was worth nothing and no better in the end than the misconduct of the younger. When the Scriptures condemn all men as sinners, that must not be interpreted as eradicating all degrees of difference among them, as placing all people upon the same level in absolute terms and denying the value and importance of living an upright life. There was a vast difference between these two sons of a common father. But the point is that it was a *relative* difference. The one lived an altogether better and more constructive life than the other, but both were sinners. And it was that which the elder brother did not understand.

Remember again that at the opening of the chapter a distinction is at once made between publicans and sinners (the prodigals) and Pharisees and scribes (the elder brothers). The people at large were held in high contempt by the Pharisaic party. 'This people', they were wont to say, 'who knoweth not the law are cursed' (John 7:49). Those for whom the rigors of the law as interpreted by the rabbis were too much the Pharisees regarded as without hope. How much more then the 'publicans and sinners'! The law was grievous to them, a burden too heavy to be borne. It was useless to them as an avenue to God, a means of salvation. They knew they could never achieve any such condition of moral and legal rectitude as would enable them to hope for eternal life.

Not so the Pharisees and scribes, however. They saw sin chiefly in quantitative terms, and regarded salvation as the

CHAPTER 10

rendering of a sufficient obedience to the law in order to
build up a surplus on the credit side. To be sure, they could
speak of grace as well. God had been gracious to his people
in giving them the law, for example. But the whole sphere
of their doctrine of salvation was one of works, of merit, of
earning the favor of God through obedience. They understood, of course, that even a Pharisee cannot be flawless in
living up to the demand of the law. But their object was to
have more acts of obedience in the ledger of God than acts
of disobedience, so that when the time came to weigh these
things out in the judgment the former would outbalance
the latter, and all would be well. Their approach here is the
very opposite of grace: it is one of contentment under legal
obligation. That is the tragedy and the horror of it. Jesus
was to tell another parable afterward which, if possible,
made even plainer still the point at issue. 'Two men went
up into the temple to pray; the one a Pharisee, and the
other a publican. The Pharisee stood and prayed thus with
himself, God, I thank thee, that I am not as other men are,
extortioners, unjust, adulterers, or even as this publican. I
fast twice in the week, I give tithes of all that I possess. And
the publican, standing afar off, would not lift up so much as
his eyes unto heaven, but smote upon his breast, saying,
God be merciful to me a sinner' (Luke 18:10-13). There it
is: the vast distinction between the two groups, between the
prodigal and the elder brother! And the Pharisee is condemned by the words of his own lips.

The elder brother was angry and would not go in. When
the father came out to entreat him, he answered, 'Lo, these
many years do I serve thee, neither transgressed I at any time
thy commandment: and yet thou never gavest me a kid,
that I might make merry with my friends'—I never behaved

as my brother has done; I have always done what you wanted, worked in the fields, obeyed your every word. 'But as soon as this thy son was come, which hath devoured thy living with harlots, thou hast killed for him the fatted calf.' His charge is one of unfairness, of a lack of consideration for faithful and diligent service, of honoring the wastrel and dissolute above the honest and upright. But his resentment at this point, his indignation at the treatment his brother received when he came home again, serves to indicate his fatal incomprehension in this whole matter. His understanding of sin was a merely quantitative one. Sin for him consisted in a series of relatively greater and lesser acts of disobedience. It was only a matter of failing to live in accordance with the comandments of God. He did not look at the heart. He was not concerned about motivation. He did not realize that while sin does relate to the quantitative, yet it is essentially qualitative. It is not merely acts of wickedness and disobedience, but a heart of rebellion against God. It had escaped him, you see, that though his prodigal brother had lived in physical estrangement from the father during the time he spent in the far country, yet he himself, living all the while in his own father's house, was no less estranged, no less in need of penitence and forgiveness and grace and restoration. And as long as he continued in that condition, with those ideas in his mind, and with that want of understanding in his heart—as long, that is, as he regarded his relationship to the father in terms of law and legal obedience—he himself, though outwardly righteous, was as dead in trespasses and sins as his openly wastrel brother had ever been.

How important it is for us to learn this lesson! You think perhaps that because you are not a drunkard or an adulterer or a thief or a liar you are as good as need be, and that when the time comes for you to die and to appear before the presence of God it will go well with you. You are not known by the name of Pharisee. No indeed! You would utterly reject being described by any such title as that. You share with others your hatred for self-righteousness and hypocrisy. Yet all unknowing you are one with the elder brother in your view of sin and the way to God. But the Scriptures declare that sin has ruined you and will prove your undoing just as much as it will any flagrant, public sinner. And you are as much in need of the grace and forgiveness of God as any prodigal.

I wish I could make clear to you that sin is not simply an act but a condition, a condition the Apostle Paul had in mind when he said, 'There is none righteous, no, not one' (Rom. 3:10). Andrew A. Bonar, one of the great Scottish preachers and spiritual writers of the nineteenth century, came from a good family, a family of ministers, a God-fearing family, and he himself was to all appearances a good and upright young man. But he had to learn to see himself as a sinner in need of grace. He wrote in his diary, shortly after he had turned nineteen—and he was never anything like a prodigal—'My birthday is past, and I am not born again. It often comes to my mind, "my friends will be for ever lost to me" for they shall be taken and I shall be left.' What searching and extraordinarily powerful words those are! That is the point to which you must come. 'I am not born again.' 'I am not born again.' Many people profess to be Christians in a general way. But how many have ever felt the searching power of that awful self-analysis: 'I am not born again'?

How dramatically Christ brings all this out in the words of

the parable itself! I suppose that from the very beginning, when he compared himself with his brother, the elder son had been possessed of a feeling of great superiority. From the earliest days of his childhood he had been in the habit of obedience. He was in every respect save one quite different from the prodigal. How he must have prided himself upon the fact that though his brother had cared nothing about the estate, about family tradition, about doing his duty, yet he, the obedient son, had given his life to these very things! There can be no question but that he held the prodigal in high contempt, the same contempt as that of the Pharisees for the people who were ignorant of the fine points of the law and who could not live as *they* did. And all through those long years, when there was no word from the far country of any change in the younger son's heart, though he doubtless commiserated with his father on the tragedy of the boy's waywardness, there was a certain feeling of satisfaction within him that he was not as his brother, that he was infinitely better and more deserving than the prodigal had ever been or could ever be. I think, too, that he rather delighted in contemplating his now exclusive position of sonship in the father's house. He, and only he, had any claim upon the father's favor and the father's goods. He was not only the elder of the two sons; because of the prodigal's rebellion he had become the only son; and all that the father had would be his.

There had, no doubt, long been tension between the two boys. We may imagine the kind of relationship they had. The very pompousness and assertive propriety of the elder brother must have aggravated the younger and made him more irresponsible still. And the very irresponsibility and carelessness of the younger brother must have caused the already considerable self-esteem and consciousness of worth in the elder to grow even more swollen. There was an inter-action here, a mutual irritation the one of the other, which pointed up and increased the bad qualities of each. But the character of the elder brother's personality was such that all he did found acceptance in the eyes of lookers-on. Was he not the very picture of loyalty, responsibility, faithfulness, obedience? Could he be faulted at any point in his life? What more could he do for his father and his father's inter-ests? We must not think that he deceived the father. No one was ever more perceptive than that father. No one ever could be. The father, after all, represents God to us. And is not God the searcher and trier of hearts? But everyone else looked up to the elder brother, respected him, took him for what he professed to be, at his word and by his example. That is not to say he was universally loved. Such people sel-dom are. But they may be highly regarded, as the Pharisees were even by those who could not imitate them or follow in their footsteps. If ever there were an upright character, attending to his duty, then it was this elder brother.

But now observe what happens. The even tenor of his days is suddenly interrupted by an unexpected event. While he was off in the fields working—he was always working, working from dawn till dusk, working as hard as he could for his father, and for himself—the prodigal came home. Throughout those worrying, suspenseful years the father had been longing for this, and the elder brother has osten-sibly longed together with him. But though the one had believed in the return and in the restoration, the other had never done so; or if he had, the return and restoration he envisaged was quite a different thing from that in the mind of his father. While he was in the fields working, the prodigal not only came home, but was greeted by the father, forgiven by the father, restored to sonship by the father, given a son's place by the father as though he had never been away. Furthermore, by the time the sun was setting and the elder brother dutifully laid down his tools and made his way home, a great celebration was underway to mark the prodigal's return and the joy of the father at having recovered his son. 'For this my son was dead, and is alive again; he was lost, and is found.' All this, mind you, without the knowledge of the diligent and faithful son. He had not been sought. He was left to toil in the field, a great feast going on at home. It seemed as though he had been left out in the cold, as though all his faithful service had been unwanted, or at any rate unappreciated; and as though the father reserved the very best he had, and all his love, for a prodigal, wastrel, ungrateful son who had flung away his substance in the far country. 'As he came and drew nigh to the house, he heard music and dancing. And he called one of the servants'—this was the first news he received of his brother's arrival—'and asked what these things meant. And he said unto him, Thy brother is come; and thy father hath killed the fatted calf, because he hath received him safe and sound.' Then, upon hearing that report, we are told, 'he was angry, and would not go in.'

As we have said, there does at first glance seem to be some legitimate cause for complaint. Any father, any Christian father, will understand the joy here at the prodigal's return. But at the same time, any diligent, dutiful person will also be able to understand the resentment which welled up in the heart of the elder brother at the excess of joy as it seemed to him which greeted his brother's arrival. But we know something now of the background against which this parable is to be interpreted. And we know also who it is that the father here represents. Hence, there can be no charge of unfairness levelled against him. It is not—of course it is not!—that he loves the wayward son and is indifferent to the faithful. That this is anything but the case may be shown by reference to the word which the father speaks to the elder brother when he comes out of the house to urge him to join in the celebration of the prodigal's return. 'Son,' he said, 'thou art ever with me, and all that I have is thine. It was meet that we should make merry, and be glad: for this thy brother was dead, and is alive again; and was lost, and is found.' No, it is not a question here of any lack of equity in the father's conduct, but rather of a lack of understanding in the mind and heart of the elder brother himself.

For whom did Christ come to die? Who are the objects of the love and the mercy of God? There is much here that is hidden in the inscrutable purposes of the heavenly Father, but it is quite clear from the New Testament, and in particular from the parable of the prodigal son, that Christ came 'to seek and to save that which was lost' (Luke 19:10). Or as he says elsewhere, 'They that be whole need not a physician, but they that are sick. But go ye and learn what that meaneth, I will have mercy, and not sacrifice: for I am not come to call the righteous, but sinners to repentance' (Matt. 9:12,13). Remember also that in this same fifteenth chapter of Luke's Gospel, at the conclusion of the parable of the lost sheep, we have Jesus' words: 'I say unto you, that likewise joy shall be in heaven over *one sinner* that repenteth, more than over ninety and nine just persons, which need no repentance' (v. 7).

What the Lord is teaching us here is not, of course, that

there are some who need his grace and power to save, and others who do not. 'All have sinned and come short of the glory of God' (Rom. 3:23). It is not his intention to contradict at one point what is clearly taught at another: namely, that there is no man or woman on earth who does not need to be saved. When he speaks of the 'whole' and the 'just' and the 'righteous,' he means those who think themselves 'whole' and 'just' and 'righteous.' And when he speaks of the 'lost' and the 'sick' and the 'sinners,' he means those who have come to see themselves as 'lost' and 'sick' and 'sinners.' That is the great distinction to be made. Precisely because the elder brother saw himself as spiritually sound and healthy, he could not grasp the reason for which the father so joyfully welcomes the prodigal home. And also because of that fancied health and righteousness of his he could not comprehend that, whatever relative superiority there may have been in his conduct over his brother's, he was as much in need of *grace* as the prodigal. No indeed, there is no such perfection in the elder of the two sons, or in any one of us, as would make it unnecessary to repent and be converted. His need, your need, my need, is the forgiving, saving, restoring grace of the Father.

> *I need thee, precious Jesus,*
> *For I am full of sin;*
> *My soul is dark and guilty,*
> *My heart is dead within.*
> *I need the cleansing fountain*
> *Where I can always flee,*
> *The blood of Christ most precious,*
> *The sinner's perfect plea.*
>
> *I need thee, precious Jesus,*
> *For I am very poor;*

A stranger and a pilgrim,
I have no earthly store.
I need the love of Jesus
To cheer me on my way,
To guide my doubting footsteps,
To be my strength and stay.

(Frederick Whitfield)

In our discussion of the second part of the parable it has become clear to us that while the prodigal himself is now bound to his father in a relationship of the freest and most perfect grace, yet the elder brother is bound to him still—in his own view and by his own desire—not in a relationship of grace, but in one of legal obligation. We must go on now to observe why it is that this striking, not to say startling, contrast has suddenly become so apparent to us. The reason surely is to be found in the *catalytic effect of conversion*. A catalyst, as we have seen, is a substance of which a small amount can promote a chemical reaction in other substances without itself undergoing permanent change or loss. Just so does the prodigal act here as a non-chemical catalyst. We see then that the presence of a gracious relationship with God in one person tends to point up its absence in others. In that sense the prodigal is a catalyst. He brings out the unconversion in his elder brother. The heart of the brother was always as it is revealed to be in this parable. He always thought of himself as whole, righteous, just; he was always confident of his standing with the father upon the ground of his own works. He had always had, underneath, a heart of resentment and rebellion. But only now, in the presence of a transformed prodigal, does his true condition appear upon the surface. In that same sense, too, any man or woman who has been genuinely converted, whose life has been transformed, who has undergone the regenerating power of the Holy Spirit, acts as a catalyst upon others, bringing to light the previously hidden resentment and ill-will and self-righteousness and sinful pride.

It is not surprising that this should be so. The Lord Jesus Christ is himself *the* catalyst of history. The Apostle Peter tells us: 'Behold, I lay in Zion a chief corner stone, elect, precious: and he that believeth on him shall not be confounded. Unto you therefore which believe he is precious: but unto them which be disobedient, the stone which the builders disallowed, the same is made the head of the corner, and a stone of stumbling, and a rock of offence, even to them which stumble at the word, being disobedient: whereunto also they were appointed' (1 Pet. 2:6-8; cf, Is. 28:16). We see thus how Christ makes a division, separating all men and women into two categories: on the one hand there are those to whom he is precious; on the other those to whom he is a stone of stumbling, and a rock of offence. And the Lord himself, using another Old Testament word (Ps. 118:22), declares: 'Did ye never read in the Scriptures, the stone which the builders rejected, the same is become the head of the corner: this is the Lord's doing, and it is marvellous in our eyes? Therefore say I unto you, The kingdom of God shall be taken from you, and given to a nation bringing forth the fruits thereof. And whosoever shall fall on this stone shall be broken: but on whomsoever it shall fall, it will grind him to powder' (Matt. 21:42-44). He, therefore, the stone, is the decisive factor in history, in the history of Israel, for the words of our Lord refer first of all to it; but then, by extension, in the history of us all. One either surrenders to his grace, or one reacts against it, to be crushed and destroyed in the end.

Now, if Christ is *the* catalyst, *the* decisive factor, of history, his people are catalysts after him. In this respect, too, the Scriptures are not silent. The Apostle Paul writes to the church at Corinth: 'Now thanks be unto God, which always causeth us to triumph in Christ, and maketh manifest the savour of his knowledge by us in every place. For we are unto God a sweet savour of Christ, in them that are saved, and in them that perish. To the one we are the savour of death unto death; and to the other the savour of life unto life. And who is sufficient for these things?' (2 Cor. 2:14-16). And the same thing is true in this second part of the parable of the prodigal son. The prodigal, now restored and forgiven, acts upon the elder brother as a savour of death. The stone wall of his righteousness now begins to show itself cracked and flawed. The merely legal basis of his relationship with the father becomes evident. Whatever else may be said of him, in the elder brother's heart there is no grace; the love of God is not in him. And what has produced the evidence of this, what has brought it out so clearly that it may be seen by all, is the presence in the father's house of the erstwhile prodigal whose life has been so radically transformed and who is now a trophy of the grace of God.

This has happened time and again throughout history where the gospel of Christ has been at work. In the very nature of the case, conversion and discipleship cannot help promoting a reaction. Sometimes that reaction is a violent one. Only think, for example, of the terrible persecutions which accompanied the spread of the church in the early centuries of her history, when the might of the Roman Empire itself—tolerant of everything else—was brought to bear upon the followers of Christ in an effort to destroy them. One remembers also the fearful sufferings of evangelical Christians at the time of the Protestant Reformation. In virtually every country where there was a return to the Scriptures and the gospel of grace, men and women laid down their lives for the sake of the Saviour of sinners. In the Low Countries thousands perished under the brutality of the soldiers of the Duke of Alva and Philip II. In England, men like Cranmer, Ridley, and Latimer were burned at the stake, so great was the hostility provoked by their evangelical confession. One recalls also the anguish of the French Huguenots in their valiant struggle for the faith, a struggle in which so great and good a man as Gaspard de Coligny was murdered for his faith. Then there are the heroic missionary martyrs, men and women who crossed wide seas and entered hostile lands in the name of the Redeemer-King and whose very presence so threatened the prevalent darkness that they were put to death. At the present time and amongst us as well, wherever the Holy Spirit is at work, when people come to Christ, there is a reaction. It is never called that. Who would not be ashamed of being thought to set himself against the truth? But opposition to the principles and the devotion and the witness of those who know Christ and the power of his resurrection is based squarely upon the very same factors which motivated the elder brother in his outburst of hostility against the prodigal son.

Modern man claims to be moved by reason, by science, by what he 'knows' empirically. And Christianity, as something he cannot know in that sense, as something which, because supernatural, is beyond the reach of his ordinary faculties, he despises as unscientific. It is not that, of course. There is nothing in the Christian faith which is contrary to true science. How could there be when the same God who has revealed himself in the Bible is also the Creator of heaven and earth, and the originator of all the laws governing what must therefore be said to be *his* creation? No, it is not that the Christian faith is unscientific which moves supposedly rational modern man to condemn and reject it. He does so for a far deeper and a far more profound reason than that. The Apostle Paul tells us what it is in those striking words of 1 Corinthians 2:14: 'But the natural man receiveth not the things of the Spirit of God: for they are foolishness unto him: neither can he know them, because they are spiritually discerned.'

Men and women today are ultimately no more scientific, no more guided by 'rationality,' than their predecessors in the past. Man is not a computer, doing his thinking after the fashion of a machine. He is a being with emotions and a will as well as an intellect. And his antipathy toward the gospel is not grounded upon the fancied irrationality of our faith, but upon his own deadness in sin. What a fearful thing it is to stand in that position and in that relationship to God! Owing him all, able to give him nothing, yet unwilling to approach him in Jesus Christ! 'He was angry, and would not go in.'

> *None other Lamb, none other Name,*
> *None other Hope in heav'n or earth or sea,*
> *None other Hiding-place from guilt and shame,*
> *None beside thee!*
>
> *My faith burns low, my hope burns low;*
> *Only my heart's desire cries out in me*
> *By the deep thunder of its want and woe,*
> *Cries out to thee!*

Lord, thou art Life, though I be dead;
Love's fire thou art, however cold I be;
Nor heav'n have I, nor place to lay my head,
Nor home, but thee!

(Christina G. Rossetti)